Preaching
and Worship in
the Small Church

Creative Leadership Series

Assimilating New Members, Lyle E. Schaller
Beginning a New Pastorate, Robert G. Kemper
The Care and Feeding of Volunteers, Douglas W. Johnson
Creative Stewardship, Richard B. Cunningham
Time Management, Speed B. Leas
Your Church Can Be Healthy, C. Peter Wagner
Leading Churches Through Change, Douglas Alan Walrath
Building an Effective Youth Ministry, Glenn E. Ludwig
Preaching and Worship in the Small Church,
William H. Willimon and Robert L. Wilson
Church Growth, Donald McGavran and George Hunter

Preaching and Worship in the Small Church

William H. Willimon & Robert L. Wilson

Creative Leadership Series

Lyle E. Schaller, Editor

Abingdon / Nashville

PREACHING AND WORSHIP IN THE SMALL CHURCH

Copyright © 1980 by Abingdon

Library of Congress Cataloging in Publication Data

WILLIMON, WILLIAM H
  Preaching and worship in the small church.
  (Creative leadership series)
  Bibliography: p.
  1. Small churches. I. Wilson, Robert Leroy,
1925–   joint author.   II. Title.   III. Series.
BV637.8.W54   253   79-24529

ISBN-0-687-33820-4

Scripture quotations are from the Revised Standard Version
of the Bible, copyrighted 1946, 1952, © 1971, 1973.

MANUFACTURED BY THE PARTHENON PRESS AT
NASHVILLE, TENNESSEE, UNITED STATES OF AMERICA

To
M. WILSON NESBITT

Pastor, Counselor, Advocate
of
Churches of Small Membership

Foreword

Approximately 60 percent of all Protestant churches in the United States and Canada contain fewer than 200 members each, and two-thirds of them average less than 120 at worship. In other words, at least one-half of all Protestant congregations on the North American continent can be classified as small.

Unlike the larger churches, which usually provide a far broader range of ministries, the small church is built around five basic components.

The first of these, and by far the most important, is "Word and Sacrament." In some parts of the land, "preaching service" is the term used to describe this regular gathering of members. Gathering together to worship God, to hear the proclamation of God's Word, and to celebrate the sacraments, are clearly the primary reasons for the existence of the small church. This is symbolized by the building, in which the largest room, and frequently the only room, is a place designed specifically for the corporate worship of God. This stands in sharp contrast to hundreds of larger churches, where less than one-half the total square footage is set apart as a place for corporate worship. It may not be a coincidence that (a) the larger the membership, the lower the proportion of members who are present for corporate worship on a typical Sunday, and (b) the larger the membership, the lower the proportion of space devoted to the function of worship and preaching of the Word.

By the design of the building, by the basic definition of the role of the minister, by the weekly schedule, and by the allocation of members' time, the small church declares that its primary reason for being is that of worship and preaching.

This also becomes the basic yardstick for the evaluation of the pastor's performance. Is the minister a good preacher? That is the number-one question in the small church. By contrast, in the larger congregations, a greater weight often is placed on the minister's capabilities as an administrator, as a creative leader, as a counselor, or as a fund raiser.

That is the basic reason this is a significant book. The authors speak directly to the most important concern of the small church. The book is directed at the first item on the agenda of the small church, and it is filled with suggestions for strengthening this vital asset.

The second distinctive component of the small congregation, and the second part of the glue that holds the small church together, is the tremendous importance of shared experience. Because it is small, all the members can know one another. To a substantial degree, larger churches are built on functions. Middle-sized churches are very dependent on the organizational and group life of the congregation. The small church is built on the relationships of members to other members. They come together at the same place to worship God, but they also come together to be with one another. "Going to church" means going both to share in a corporate worship experience and to be with the other persons who constitute that particular called-out community. Here is a simple example of the emphasis that people in small churches place on shared experience: the funeral service for someone from a thousand-member church often will be attended by fewer than a hundred persons, but twice that number may appear for the funeral service of one of the eighty-member congregation.

That is the second reason this is an important book.

Willimon and Wilson explain why the Lord's Supper, baptisms, weddings, and funerals, are essential shared events in the lives of the people in the small congregation. Three chapters are devoted to ways the pastor and the lay leaders can increase the effectiveness of the church's ministry in these shared experiences.

The third part of the glue that holds the small church together, and perhaps its most distinctive characteristic, is the prominence of the laity. Most small congregations are controlled by the laity. The larger the membership, the more influential the role of the pastor. In the small church, however, the laity gives each congregation its individual identity. Willimon and Wilson have caught this concept and reflected it authentically. The unique role of the laity in the small church comes through very clearly, especially in chapters 3, 7, and 9.

The Sunday school and the attachment to a particular place are the other two basic components of the typical small church. Throughout the narrative the authors affirm the significance of that meeting place and repeatedly lift up the centrality of the educational ministry, whether it be through preaching, through reeducating the people on the importance of the Lord's Supper, or through the more intentional use of meaningful symbols.

This is an affirming book. It affirms the role and the basic values of the small church. It affirms the centrality of Word and Sacrament. It affirms the role of the pastor of the small congregation. It affirms the laity and their values. On this foundation of authentic affirmation can be built creative and inspiring ministries, as the laity and the minister serve God together, in and through the small church.

Lyle E. Schaller
Yokefellow Institute

Contents

Introduction   13

I   Where Few Are Gathered   18

II   Thinking Small   29

III   The Lord's Day   37

IV   The Service of Worship   47

V   The Lord's Supper: Mealtime in the Family   63

VI   Baptism: The Family Claims Its Own   79

VII   Weddings and Funerals:
Crisis Within the Family   92

VIII   Preaching in the Small Church:
Serving the Word   101

IX   Lay Reaction to Preaching:
Receiving the Word   110

X   Servants of the Word   119

Suggestions for Further Reading   125

Introduction

The names have a strange, almost quaint sound in the urban and technological society of this last quarter of the twentieth century. Some, like Antioch, Hebron, Shiloh, and Mt. Bethel, remind us that biblical places were more familiar to Christian people of earlier generations than they are to church members today. Other names are reminiscent of a rural America long past: Pleasant Green, Piney Grove, Gravel Hill, and Harmony Valley. Some carry the names of people, possibly the founders—Burton Memorial—or a still-prominent family—Walker's Chapel.

We are speaking of the small-membership church, an institution which has had and continues to have a significant influence on the lives of millions of Americans. At least one such church, and usually several, can be found in virtually every community in the land. These congregations are numbered, not in the thousands, but in the tens of thousands. It would not be an overstatement to say that the small church is still the predominant form of institution in American Protestantism.

Although the popular image of the small church is rural, and the vast majority of such congregations are in sparsely populated areas, not all are. Many are located in urban centers. Small struggling Protestant congregations with modest buildings can be found in hundreds of residential neighborhoods in cities across the nation; scores of storefront churches are located in the inner-city communities of every major metropolitan center.

"Ambivalent" is the word that describes the feelings of church people toward the congregation of small membership. Many see it through the rose-colored glasses of nostalgia and long wistfully for a return to a past that never really existed—a world of pastoral purity, where the little brown (or white) church in the vale was the center of community life. These same people also have a gnawing feeling that the small church is somehow second-rate and does not quite measure up to what it ought to be in today's world.

Other persons, particularly the clergy and denominational leaders, view the small church as an anachronism, kept alive by stubborn people who are holding on to an institution that should be allowed or even encouraged to die. They see such churches as impediments to the development of the kind of congregation needed today. In the meantime the small congregation continues to exist, doing what it and the Christian Church have always done, albeit imperfectly: winning adherents, nurturing them in the Christian way of life, gathering them each week for worship and preaching, and in many rural communities, finally burying them in the adjacent cemetery, confident that they have successfully run the race and received the reward of the faithful.

This is a book about worship and preaching in churches of small membership—those congregations with two hundred or fewer persons on the roll. Between one-half and two-thirds of all Protestant churches fall into this category. Furthermore, when the inaccuracies of church rolls and the number of nonresident members are taken into consideration, it will be noted that the two hundred persons reported in the denominational year book actually represent a lesser number of active participants. It also indicates a typical Sunday worship service with fewer than seventy-five persons present.

This book will consider the nature of such churches and the reasons they are so durable, seeming to defy the attempts of clergy and denominational officials to change them. The major focus will be on the thing the church of small membership does best: it provides a Christian community where the people participate in worship, hear the Word, and carry on a ministry to one another and to the larger community.

There are four reasons we felt this book was necessary. The first is the way church leaders have attempted to deal with the perceived "problem" of the small congregation by trying to make it into a large organization through merger or some type of parish arrangement. In both instances the model is the large church, the small congregation being pressured to become what it generally cannot be.

The second reason is the frequent disregard of the significance of preaching, and especially worship, in contemporary thought on the practice and theology of the ordained ministry. Many pastors now seem to feel that most of their efforts in either the church or the community are more important than preaching and worship. While this oversight is tragic for the church in general, it is particularly tragic for the small church. In the preaching/worship event, churches of small membership may recover their unique identity and mission to the world, as well as their particular contribution to the larger body of Christ.

The third is that ministers need to better understand the nature of the small church and its ministry. Given the large number of such congregations, many clergy will spend a portion, if not all, of their ministry in such churches. If they

15

are going to achieve an effective ministry and find satisfaction in their calling, it will be within the context of the church of small membership.

The fourth and perhaps the most important reason is that lay members need to realize that the small church can be an effective instrument of ministry, particularly through worship and preaching. The lay people always have known that worship and preaching are central; otherwise they would not have continued to attend, week after week. By better understanding the nature of worship and preaching, lay people will not only have their long-standing faith in these activities affirmed, but they will find their own Sunday morning experience enriched and more meaningful.

The small church is not without its share of problems. Nevertheless, as an institution, it is going to be with us for the indefinite future. Only by realistically understanding its strengths and weaknesses, its problems and potential, can the lay members and clergy help it to carry on the most effective ministry possible. If this book makes some contribution to that ministry, it will have achieved its purpose.

A large number of persons and several organizations have made significant contributions to this study. Since it was founded over a half century ago, the Office of Rural Church Affairs of the Duke Endowment has worked with hundreds of rural churches in North Carolina on building programs, parish development, and leadership training. Albert F. Fisher and M. Wilson Nesbitt of the Duke Endowment staff have provided invaluable assistance in the preparation of this book by making their files available and by critiquing the research. The support by the Duke

Endowment of the J. M. Ormond Center has made possible additional research on small congregations. We are particularly indebted to John K. Bergland for his assistance with the chapters on preaching. The Divinity School students who serve as pastors and workers in churches of small membership shared their experiences and insights. Anne Daniels, secretary in the J. M. Ormond Center, typed the manuscript. The data on the lay reaction to preaching were gathered with the assistance of a grant from the Reserve for Religious Research, administered by the General Council on Ministries of the United Methodist Church.

It is our hope that this book will be helpful to the members and pastors of small churches, as they witness and minister in their communities across the land.

Chapter One
Where Few Are Gathered

Donald Sheldon is in his fourth year as pastor of the Mt. Bethel and Centerville congregations, two small churches in the Midwest. It is his first position since his graduation from theological school. He has recently been approached by a large church about becoming their assistant pastor. He does not really want to accept the position, but he is reluctant to turn it down. In discussing the matter with a ministerial colleague, he said, "I like working with the people at Mt. Bethel and Centerville; they are dedicated Christians. They want me to stay. However, neither church is going to grow, and they are already paying me about what they can afford. My friends tell me I'm wasting my talents by staying with these small churches. I would prefer to remain, but I am concerned about the effect on my career if I turn down this invitation."

Donald Sheldon's dilemma illustrates the enigma of the small church. These congregations need pastors but can afford only modest salaries. The success of a minister is determined by his or her ability to move to larger congregations. In a society that values growth and size, the small church remains the same; it does not grow and it refuses to die. It continues year after year, seeming to change little, if at all.

There are three types of small churches. The first is the newly organized congregation which, while now small, is growing or is expected to grow. In the foreseeable future such churches will become large. The second is the declining congregation, one that once was large but has decreased in membership so that it now can be classified as small. Some of these churches will eventually go out of existence.

The third type is the congregation that has always been small and will remain so for the indefinite future; this type constitutes the majority of small churches. Many are located in rural areas that do not have large populations. Others are in cities, where the reason for their failure to grow must be other than the availability of people. Some are relatively new churches, organized with the expectation that they would increase in size, but which for some reason have remained small.

The preponderance of small churches in Protestantism can be illustrated by examining denominational statistics. In 1976 The United Methodist Church reported 7,069 congregations with fewer than 50 members, or 18 percent of the total. There were 15,742 churches, or 41 percent, with a membership of less than 100. A total of 24,855 churches had fewer than 200 persons on the rolls, a figure representing 64 percent of all of the congregations. The almost two-thirds of United Methodist congregations with fewer than 200 members contain about one-fourth of that denomination's total membership. Another example is the Lutheran Church of America, where 13 percent of the congregations have fewer than 100 confirmed members, and one-third have fewer than 190. Among the congregations affiliated with the National Association of Congregational Christian Churches, 18 percent have fewer than 100 members, and 41 percent list fewer than 200 persons on the church roll. And 62 percent of the congregations in the Southern Baptist Convention have fewer than 300 members.

Small congregations mean that there will be few persons at worship services. The United Methodist Church provides data on the average attendance at the principal weekly service. In 3,872 churches (10 percent) the average attendance is less than 20. There are 9,668 churches (26 percent) with an average of fewer than 35 persons in attendance and 15,013 (57 percent) with an average attendance of less than 75 at the principal service. These data illustrate that many sermons are preached regularly to a relatively small group of people.

Basic Assumptions

The first basic assumption underlying this book is that the Christian gospel can be communicated effectively and that persons can respond positively in a wide range of institutional settings. Throughout Christian history, the primary institution for carrying and celebrating the gospel has been the parish church, which has been and continues to be one of society's most durable institutions. There has been a wide range of types of local churches as people of different social, economic, and cultural groups respond to the gospel and form institutions where they witness to their faith and nurture believers.

There is no one kind of congregation that at all times and in all settings has been the most effective or the most Christian. Churches of all sizes, with many different styles of program, have existed and will continue to exist. There is no theological reason causing the large church to be any more or less effective than the small. However, a variety of other reasons may make the large congregation desirable. These may be cultural, such as having enough people to form a large choir, in order to sing certain types of music. There may be management reasons—more people provide a larger income. There may be sociological reasons, such as maintaining large youth groups so that the teen-agers may have more persons to date. However, there is no reason the *theological purposes* of the church cannot be fulfilled as well in a small, as in a large congregation.

The second assumption is that the small church is going to be an integral part of Protestantism for a long time. The large number of such churches would seem to make this inevitable. A significant proportion of jobs for clergy are and will continue to be in these congregations.

It is not an exaggeration to say that most ministers will be involved with small churches during a part, if not all, of their professional careers. These churches will not vanish; the clergy and the denominational leaders will be obliged to continue to give attention to them. How church leaders deal with such congregations will do much to determine the effectiveness of the ministry of both the congregations and the clergy.

Perceptions of the Small Church

The small church is a problem primarily for the clergy, and especially for denominational officials. For the clergy, the problem is related to income and status. Pastors are employed by churches, and large congregations have more money and pay higher salaries. And people, including clergy, find high salaries more desirable than low ones.

The individual's status, to a large degree, is determined by the institution to which he or she is related. Thus the professor at a prestigious Ivy League school will have higher status than the teacher in a midwestern community college. The pastor of a large urban congregation will be ranked higher by his or her peers than will the minister serving three small rural churches.

The status a particular church affords its pastor is determined by the way the church is perceived by the pastor's professional peers. The Christian church has always been able to recruit persons for difficult positions which not only require self-sacrifice but offer little in material rewards. Foreign missionaries are examples: their assignments are demanding, they are separated from their families, and the pay is meager. But the missionary is seen as a member of an elite corps of Christians, a kind of spiritual Green Beret. A description of the annual commissioning service held by a denominational mission board for persons being sent overseas shows the esteem in which they were held. The auditorium would be packed. On the stage were the missionary candidates, clad in white robes. The bishop, an eloquent preacher, would tell the new missionaries that they were following in the footsteps of St. Paul by carrying the gospel into the difficult parts of the world—that the entire church supported them and was proud of them. It was heady stuff. When they arrived at their small congregations in the Peruvian Andes or in central Africa, they certainly did not feel like failures, nor were they perceived as such. Contrast this with the pastor of three small churches in Georgia or Minnesota, who may be seen, not as someone dedicating his or her life to the glorious task of preaching the gospel, but as one who can't make it in the ecclesiastical employment system.

Denominational officials see the small church from their own unique perspective. If their job includes the placement of clergy, they must locate pastors who can be persuaded to accept such churches. If their task is primarily the operation of mission and benevolent programs, they are aware that the small church can provide only a modest amount of funds, and often requires subsidy itself. Small churches may consume a large amount of an administrator's time, but contribute relatively little to the benevolent programs so dear to the hearts of denominational officials.

Many lay persons in small congregations have come to accept the idea that their churches are, in fact, inferior to larger ones. The pastors and judicatory officials communicate this to the lay members in various ways. It is generally recognized that a promotion for a minister means moving from a smaller to a larger congregation. When the pastor of a small church receives an advancement, he or she moves to a larger congregation. How does it affect the attitude of the members, if the new pastor is perceived as someone who is being demoted or is obviously a new and inexperienced seminary graduate?

A typical case is that of a young graduate who accepted four small churches. There was an understanding between the pastor and the people that he would stay four years, although there was no contract. At the end of the second year the minister had an opportunity to move to a church in the city. The attitude of the people toward their pastor and themselves was expressed by a local church official who said, "We are sorry to see John leave, but we don't want to stand in the way of his getting a promotion."

When a pastor moves from a larger to a smaller church, at worst, he will be perceived as being punished for some misconduct, and at best, as being incompetent. This point can be illustrated by the case of an experienced minister who voluntarily left a large congregation to accept an appointment to a rural parish consisting of four small churches. Several months later he was visited by a leading layman from his former congregation. During the course of the evening the layman said, "You may not want to answer this, but what did you do that the bishop sent you here to these churches?"

The prevailing attitude among lay people, clergy, and denominational officials is that small churches are inferior churches.

Weaknesses and Strengths

The church of small membership has both weaknesses and strengths that are the direct result of membership size. The resources of a small group are limited when compared to those of a large one. The programs that can be carried on with fifty persons will, of course, be more modest than those possible with five hundred people. The special interest and age groupings, such as study classes; men's, women's, and youth organizations; or Sunday school classes paralleling those in the public school, are not possible in the small church. The building will tend to provide only limited facilities, thus placing further restriction on possible programs.

If there is a choir, the range of anthems will be limited. A small electronic organ or piano, rather than a grand pipe organ, will accompany congregational singing. Elaborately printed bulletins for worship services may be unaffordable or impractical. If a pastor is shared with other congregations, it may be difficult to plan worship and preaching with the needs of one particular congregation in mind. In fact, if the pastor is forced to divide time between a number of congregations or find other part-time employment, he or she may feel there is never enough time for careful, reflective, long-range planning of preaching and worship. Members of small churches, when comparing their worship services with the carefully orchestrated, "professionally" led music, preaching, and worship of larger churches, often receive the distinct impression that their worship is second-rate, amateurish, and only a pale image of the real thing.

Finances are a perennial problem. The small congregation tends to spend a large proportion of its income (often between one-half and two-thirds) for pastoral services. Even then, it generally shares the pastor with one or more other churches, or it employs a part-time minister who also holds a secular job.

The denomination has a range of expectations for the local congregation. These include a form of internal organization with various committees, commissions, and offices, certain prescribed programs for the different age groups, and a tax which the congregation is expected to contribute to certain mission projects and denominational programs. Many churches of small membership simply cannot meet these expectations. There are not enough people to staff the committees or participate in the programs. The "fair share" of the denominational budget may leave the congregation little for programs, after the pastor is paid and the necessary expenses of operating the church, such as utilities and Sunday school literature, are met.

The small-membership church has certain strengths, however, sometimes overlooked in a mass society that emphasizes growth and bigness. In the small congregation, each individual is vital to the organization. The group needs each participant; everyone is aware when someone is absent. The proportion of members present for worship in small churches is typically higher than in larger ones.

The reason is obvious: every person is needed, and each absentee knows he or she will be missed. The individual cannot be anonymous in the small church.

A larger proportion of the members of a small congregation participate in the management of the church. In the large church, only a small proportion may be on the governing board; a small church may operate as a committee of the whole. As a result, persons in such congregations tend to have a strong sense of responsibility for, and ownership of, their church and its activities.

Members of small congregations may develop a strong sense of community. Such a group can provide an effective support for its members, functioning as a kind of extended family. We shall be using the analogy of the family as worship and preaching are discussed. There is, however, a danger that small churches can become exclusive and reluctant to accept the newcomer or willing to do so only after the individual has undergone something similar to a probationary period.

Worship and preaching are central to the life of any small congregation. Without the claim of a large youth group, graded Sunday school classes, magnificent facilities, a large budget with a host of benevolent causes, or a weekly round of activities for all age groups, the *raison d'être* for most small churches is the Sunday morning worship service. There may be small churches without a building, without an educational program, without a budget, and without formal organizational structure, but there are no small churches without preaching and worship. We consider this a positive advantage of the small church, which can help it to remember—amidst the current emphasis upon church organizational tinkering and maintenance, educational programs, counseling services, social activities, and community service—that the primary ministry of God's church, from which all other ministries are derived, is the ministry of Word and Sacrament—the proclamation, prayer, and praise of the Lord who calls us together and sends us forth.

In the light of current liturgical studies, new perspectives on preaching, and recent innovations in worship, the very smallness of the small church can be seen as a distinct advantage for preaching and worship. The homelike setting of these churches, the close relationship that can exist between the preacher/worship leader and the people, the often high level of participation among the worshipers, the lack of anonymity, the sense of community, the awareness of individual needs, are all positive characteristics as far as preaching and worship are concerned. In the next chapters of this book we hope to demonstrate why an understanding of its particular character, when coupled with an understanding of the purpose, practice, and theology of Christian preaching and worship, can result in a fresh, positive look at the possibilities for the life and liveliness of the small church—possibilities that may far outweigh the problems of these important, but often neglected, parts of the body of Christ.

Impact of the Small Church

In December of 1944, the German army launched an unexpected attack. In what was to become known as the Battle of the Bulge, a deep salient was driven in the Allied lines. Writing in *World War II* about the reaction of the American troops to this attack, James Jones said:

> No one of these little road junction stands could have had a profound effect on the German drive. But

27

hundreds of them, impromptu little battles at
nameless bridges and unknown crossroads, had an
effect of slowing enormously the German im-
petus. . . . These little die-hard "one-man-stands,"
alone in the snow and fog without communications,
would prove enormously effective out of all proportion to their size. (p. 205)

Perhaps there is a parable here. The kingdom is advanced
significantly, not by what takes place in the denominational headquarters, but by the ministry in local congregations in communities across the nation, including the
churches of small membership. The results are enormously effective, out of all proportion to their size.

Chapter Two
Thinking Small

A lay member of a small church seeking a pastor was discussing a candidate with a judicatory official: "Even if this minister comes to our church, he won't stay long. He is an able young man who will soon move on to a bigger church, one that can pay a salary larger than we can provide. No one wants to stay at a small church."

There is something in American culture that tends to place a high value on growth and size. We take pride in a thing that is the largest of its kind, whether it be an airplane or an office building, or a church. A town experiencing a rapid increase of population will put up a billboard in a prominent place, proclaiming that it is the fastest-growing community in the state. Why we are this way is difficult to explain. It may be related to the fact that the United States is still a relatively young nation, and the push to settle and develop the country has left so deep an impression on us that we are still attempting to achieve these already-realized goals. Whatever the reason, to grow and to become larger is considered good; to remain stable or to decrease in size is not desirable.

The same attitude prevails among Protestant churches. If membership is increasing, if budgets and the amounts contributed to denominational mission causes are escalating, there is reason for rejoicing. If the opposite is true, the result is concern, and even anguish, among church leaders.

Progress in the local church tends to be determined by growth and to be measured by statistical indicators. The forms that pastors of some denominations are required to complete annually contain, in addition to items such as membership and attendance, the amount of funds contributed by the congregations to a multiplicity of denominational programs. If the figures are going up, the congregation and its pastor are presumed to be succeeding. If they are remaining the same or decreasing, something is obviously wrong.

We would argue that local churches should attempt to evaluate their effectiveness as objectively as possible. Unfortunately, much of the data gathered by denominations does not contribute to such an evaluation but is primarily to remind the congregation to contribute more. One denomination required each pastor to report the number of subscriptions to a church magazine purchased by the parishioners, and these figures then appeared in the yearbook. The publishing agency with its sophisticated computer did not need this information; it knew how many copies were sold. The purpose of the question was to remind the minister to persuade more of the members to subscribe.

Apart from the general acceptance of the standards in American culture, the question can be raised as to whether there are reasons within the church that reinforce its acceptance of the values of growth and size. The presuppositions that provided the rationale for the Protestant churches' understanding of their nature and role in society in the past two decades have contributed to the downgrading of the small church.

Internal Obstacles
Two internal denominational factors have contributed to the feeling among those persons associated with small

churches that their congregations are less than adequate. The first is the emphasis that has been given to involvement of the church in working for social change. The second is the concept of the ideal local congregation, held as normative by the denominational agencies.

In the late 1950s the denominational emphasis began to shift from the development of new churches and traditional missional and congregational activities to problems in the larger society. The shift was gradual during the early years of the 1960s, but by mid-decade, the emphasis was concentrated on the civil rights movement. This was the period of protests throughout the South and urban riots in the cities of the North and West.

The really significant activity for church leaders was not in carrying out the traditional ministries that had always occupied congregations, but in being a part of the protest marches and helping to correct the evils in society. It was during those times that the Stated Clerk of the United Presbyterian Church was arrested while attempting to integrate an amusement park in Maryland, and a black and a white bishop together were refused admission to a church in Mississippi. It was clear to everyone that social action was the real ministry of the church.

The analysis of the wisdom and the effectiveness of the churches' part in the social movements of the 1960s and 70s is not the concern of this book. The point is that for an institution to influence the larger society, it must have numerical strength. The small congregation by itself cannot have any great influence on the complex problems in the larger society. Thus its weakness, if not irrelevance (it could still contribute money), was accentuated.

Probably more important, the social-action ministries were almost always outside the congregation. The pastor whose main interest was winning adherents to the church and nurturing them in the faith was perceived as not being devoted to the real mission of the church. The issues receiving the attention and energy of the denominations were thought to be more important. While there are evils in the society that desperately need to be corrected, we would argue that identifying this as the only, or even the primary, task of the church had a negative impact on the congregations, particularly in the small churches. The effect was to communicate to such congregations that what they did, and often did very well, was not what the church was all about.

The same trend continues as the denominational agencies remind their constituencies that their efforts should be focused on such issues as colonialism, the multinational corporations, world hunger, majority rule in Rhodesia, racism, minority empowerment, and the criminal justice system. The result is that people, and particularly the pastor in the small church, feel overwhelmed and frustrated because they cannot address themselves to those issues their denominational leaders tell them are most important.

Denominations tend to have expectations for every congregation that are beyond the capabilities of many small churches. The number of officials and committees necessary for each congregation reminds the members that their church is below par. In a typical small one-room rural church, there was posted on the rear wall a typed list of all the congregational officials the denomination required. Many names appeared more than once. That church of forty-eight members did not have so complex an organization. The letter of the law was being followed, and the people again were being reminded that they were not as adequate as a local church should be.

The numerous programs promoted by the various units of the denominational bureaucracies, which exist for that purpose, also contribute to the feeling of inferiority among members of small churches. They cannot have the missions programs; the social-action projects; the programs for women, men, youth, and children; the study groups; or the evangelistic campaigns considered essential for a "full church program." Thus the members of churches of small membership continue to gather for worship, preaching, and nurture, but under the cloud of a feeling of inadequacy.

Where to Begin

It is not enough to determine that the small church is perceived by many clergy and lay people to be a less-than-adequate congregation and to explain why this is so. It is also necessary to consider what might be done to alter this situation. To change the negative image of the small-membership church, persons at all levels of the denomination must rethink the mission and the ministry of the congregation. This will not be an easy task; change tends to come slowly, especially when we are not quite sure we want to change.

Essential to any process of desired change is the acceptance of the small church as it is, with both its strengths and its weaknesses. There is a tendency among Protestant clergy to want to remodel their congregations. Pastors sometimes try to remake the small church into their concept of what a church ought to be, which in most cases is a large church. The ideal church may not exist in reality, but only in the minister's imagination.

The question the pastor needs to ask is not How can I change this congregation? but How can I assist the small church to witness and minister as effectively as possible? To answer this latter question, several factors need to be considered.

One error is the tendency to see the characteristics cherished by the members of the small church as manifestations of the people's lack of vision, misinterpretation of the gospel, and sinfulness in general. Thus its stability is seen as inertia, the congregation's concern with their heritage as "living in the past," and the strong fellowship as a closed clique. While these descriptions may apply to some church groups, they are not necessarily characteristic of small congregations in general.

A young pastor commented, "I don't want to stay long at Bethany; it is a church that is not going anywhere." He was correct, if by "not going anywhere" he meant that the membership would not increase drastically, a new building would not be built, and that no new or different programs would be initiated. Bethany would continue to be a traditional church where people gather to worship and hear the Word, to nurture and support one another. The pastor's concern seemed to be that the church was not going to change in ways that would enhance his career. Bethany was an effective church from the perspective of the members who worshiped there and supported it; they could see no reason to change. The pastor, however, could not be satisfied with what he perceived as a routine, static, congregation.

Another issue is the church's relationship to the larger community, as perceived by the congregation. The contemporary church accepts as axiomatic the statement that a primary purpose of the church is to serve the

34

community. This assumption needs to be questioned. The primary task of the church is to *create* a sense of community. If the congregation develops into a Christian community, it will be able to witness and minister. It can be supportive of individuals in their time of stress and difficulty. It can reach out to persons outside the group and bring them inside, making them a part of the fellowship.

Therefore, the question churches tend to ask, How can we serve the community? is the wrong question. The church, and particularly the small church, needs instead to ask, How can we *create* community? If the community is not developed, not effective in its witness to the faith, not adequate in the care of its members, and unconcerned about its outreach, the group of people meeting in a building with a spire and stained-glass windows is not a church.

Another issue is the difference in the way lay people and clergy perceive the small church. Carl S. Dudley, in his insightful book, *Making the Small Church Effective,* has compared the small congregation to a single-cell organism. Such an organism has a life different from that of a multicell organism, but an existence, nevertheless. The members of the small church find it worthwhile; otherwise they would not continue to attend it. Judging by the loyalty many persons demonstrate, they do find membership meaningful.

But while the members may view small churches as satisfactory and meaningful, many pastors do not. As has been shown, the small congregation cannot provide the institutional support that meets the clergy's career expectations. Indeed, the small church may be able to provide a minimal level of support, which will enable only a part-time pastor to be employed.

There is no simple solution, and in many cases there may be no completely satisfactory solution. The needs of full-time professional clergy cannot be met by many churches of small membership. It is essential to realize that this issue exists, but that the institutional limitations of the small church do not prevent it from being a valid instrument of witness and ministry.

The small-membership church may be somewhat analogous to an extended family. It is a group that continues over time, in some cases, for an entire lifetime. It has a heritage that gives the members a sense of identity—of knowing who they are. It celebrates the members' victories and supports them in times of difficulty. It develops rituals that mark the changes in life patterns. There may be internal tension and conflict, but it closes ranks when any member is threatened by external forces. It can be caring and loving, but it can discipline the member who deviates from its norms. It may be difficult or impossible to join. The individual cannot join a family; he or she has to be adopted. The same is true of many small churches; here the individual does not join, but is adopted. Once received into the family, however, the person is an integral part of it and shares fully in the rights and obligations of the group.

To begin to "think small"—that is, positively—about the church of small membership, we must begin with a reexamination of the effect of these congregations on the lives of their people and of the relation of this effect to the purpose of the Christian church. This means considering the way the theological understanding of the church is manifested in a social setting. The manner in which small churches perform this function is the subject to which we now turn.

Chapter Three
The Lord's Day

It is early on Sunday morning. A bright winter sun beams its first rays upon Bethel Church. A pickup truck arrives. A man gets out, unlocks the front door of the little church and enters. He is George Smith. Every Sunday at this time George comes to the church, turns on the heat or opens the windows, according to the season, then returns home for breakfast before time for church. Some time later a car arrives, and Mrs. Lucy Thompson enters the church and goes back to the adult Sunday school room behind the sanctuary. As usual, she places her lesson notes on the lectern, arranges the ten chairs in a semicircle, then sits down to await the first class members. Her wait is not long, for soon two more cars roll into the parking lot, and the Johnsons and the Tates enter the church. About 10:00, a station wagon rumbles into the lot, and six or seven young people, ranging in age from twelve to seventeen, get out of the car and enter the sanctuary, where their Sunday school class meets. Four more cars arrive in rapid succession, bringing the number of people now at church to about twenty-four. Singing is heard in the adult Sunday school room; Mrs. Cline has just started to read a Bible story to the three children in her class; and the teen-agers are talking about yesterday's football game with Mr. Evans. Sunday school is in session.

At about 10:45, the classes end, the women take seats in the sanctuary to chat, Clara Brown arranges a vase of fall leaves upon the altar, the men cluster around the oak tree in front of the church to smoke and talk, the young people gather to look at Mr. Evans' new car, and Mrs. Cline helps little Sally Evans pin her picture of the good Samaritan on the wall of the Sunday school room. Three more carloads of people arrive, one bearing old John Jacobs, who is now out of the hospital after his operation, and everyone goes to greet him and help him up the steps. A small car skids to a stop next to the front door. "Here's the preacher," shouts one of the children. Jim Morris, a young man in his late twenties, gets out of the car, and one of the youth carries his robe in as Jim shakes hands with a few of the men. Bethel Church shares Jim with Oak Ridge Church, a few miles down the road.

The men and youth filter into the sanctuary. Mrs. Thompson sits down at the piano, while George, James, Louise, and Mary take their places in the choir. Mrs. Thompson plays a few bars from a hymn, Jim Morris enters in his robe, walks to the pulpit, opens his hymnal, and says, "Good morning. Let us worship God." The congregation responds, "Good morning."

Sunday is happening at Bethel Chuch.

What Happened to Sunday?

When the earliest Christians gathered, unlike their Jewish forebears who remembered the sabbath and kept it holy, they chose to gather on Sunday, the Lord's Day, as they called it. Sunday, the first day of the week, was seen by them as a Resurrection Day, the first day of the New Age, the sign of God's near and active presence as the Risen Christ in their community. The heart of their faith, the significance of the gospel, the meaning of their fellowship, was signified by Sunday. That day was central.

Through an odd set of diverse historical circumstances, Sunday eventually declined somewhat as the focal point of life within the church. In the Roman church, the centrality of Sunday was obscured by a host of saints' days, major feasts during the week, and by a proliferation of weekday masses. Protestants generally did not suffer from these problems, since a major goal of the Reformers was to restore Sunday to its position as *the* major occasion in the life of a congregation, by eliminating the competing worship services and saints' days. It was hoped that Sunday—the day of the Resurrection, the feast of the Incarnation, the celebration of the Atonement—would be seen as the goal and the source of all other congregational activities.

But in our own century, the centrality of Sunday has been threatened in other ways. Protestant churches fostered Sunday evening services, worship in Sunday school, Wednesday night prayer meetings and other services that tended to either duplicate Sunday morning worship, or even improve upon it (in emotional intensity, singing of the "good old hymns," lay participation, and informality), as far as many lay people were concerned. Also, Sunday worship became the victim of the "full-program church" mentality. When asked, "Who is a Christian?" the Protestant lay person who responded, "A Christian is someone who goes to church on Sunday," was quickly informed that that was only a small part of the Christian life. "What you do outside the church is more important than what you do inside the church," was how the slogan went. Church school classes, youth-fellowship meetings, weekly prayer and Bible study groups, social-action programs, elaborately designed educational activities, and seemingly endless committee meetings, all conspired to convince people that worship was only one small part of the full program.

Such thinking had an undeniable appeal to the pragmatic, utilitarian, work-oriented society, such as we have in the United States. Time spent in worship tends to be thought of as idle time—unused time. We are a nation of doers and achievers. How can the "acts" of worship compete in importance alongside activities such as Christian education, counseling, youth programs, board meetings, Bible study groups, and charitable work? The "active" church with its doors always open, meetings in progress every night of the week, newsletters recruiting participants for a host of activities, insuring that every person is kept busy throughout the week (provided that person truly wishes to be an "active" church member), has become the paradigm for any church that aspires to greatness. The "active" pastor, with a full round of weekly meetings, community activities, and supervisory chores, which keep all the machinery oiled and running smoothly at the full-program church (provided that church truly wishes to be a "viable" church), has become the paradigm for any pastor who aspires to greatness. Somehow the centrality of Sunday worship has been lost amidst these pragmatic, program-oriented, organizational images of success.

A Christian Goes to Church on Sunday

For the majority of Christians, and for much of the history of the church, being a Christian has been best described as "going to church on Sunday." In itself, by the very nature of its purpose and significance, Sunday is a biblical and theological statement of who Christians are, what Christian worship is about, and what the church is called to do. When the old catechism spoke of the "chief end of man" as being "to glorify God and enjoy him forever"; when the Reformers spoke of the church as the place where "the Word is rightly proclaimed and the sacraments are duly administered"; when Paul spoke of a gathering of Christians as being "the body of Christ" (I Cor. 12:27), they were all declaring the same thing Sunday worship declares. The primary focus and reason for our worship is God. We worship simply because God is God and because we are God's children. Growth (statistical or spiritual), social change, organizational maintenance, therapeutic benefits, education, and so on, are always secondary—possible spinoffs from the central activity of worshiping God. And while the chief end of worship is the glorification of God and nothing else, it is also true that even as we are busy serving God in our service of worship, we find that we and our needs are being graciously served *by* God when we worship. But without the worship, there is no assurance that the good we do inside or outside the church is *God's* good, and we have no right to claim that even the most noble of the activities in which a church may engage are part of *God's* activity.

Small churches may not be able to fit some of our current images of ecclesiastical success; they may not be able to meet whatever organizational requirements may be placed upon them by their various denominations; they may fail in their attempts to provide even the vaguest semblance of the full-program church. But, to our knowledge, there are no small churches that do not do a reasonably good job of celebrating Sunday. In fact, some small churches celebrate Sunday in a fashion that puts many of their larger sister churches to shame.

Small churches that measure themselves by the standards of that elusive thing called the full-program church, or that buy into some of the currently popular concepts of the viable organization, are doomed to continuing frustration. We are in an odd situation indeed when a Christian church is made to feel inadequate because the only reason it exists is for worship on Sunday. To return to an earlier point, one basis for the centrality of Sunday is that Sunday worship so beautifully signifies and makes visible the theological purpose of the church and its ministry. One suspects that some more active churches immerse themselves in a dizzying array of basketball games, bazaars, field trips, study groups, community services, and organizational maintenance, in a subtle attempt to avoid coming to terms with the basic theological purpose of the church. Even the worship services of those churches frequently have a breathless, hurried, distracted quality. The busy, thriving, suburban church, whose program and activities are scarcely distinguishable from those of the neighborhood Y.M.C.A., and whose pastor appears to be little more than a program director for a community club, is in a more dangerous situation than it cares to admit. Theologians have long noted that our Pelagian busyness is frequently a works/righteousness cover-up for our spiritual emptiness.

Small churches will recover their own unique sense of mission and will restore their positive self-image only when they recover and boldly claim the fundamental significance of Sunday for their congregational life and for the life of the universal church. Small churches may not be equipped to do some of the jobs larger churches have taken upon themselves in recent years, but they are fully prepared to proclaim and to celebrate the Word, to care for and edify the body of Christ, and to foster, in Richard

Niebuhr's memorable phrase, an "increase of the love of God and neighbor." The fulfillment of the theological purpose of the church never requires a crowd.

Specifically, this means that pastors of small-membership churches will need to view preaching and worship leadership as their primary pastoral activities. This makes not only good theological sense, but also good practical sense. In that Sunday morning gathering, a pastor is with, and facing, more of his or her parishioners for a longer, more focused, and intentional time than on any other occasion during the week. It would be foolish for any pastor to treat such an occasion lightly. Careful planning of the services, skillful preparation of the sermons, and the constant reevaluation and refinement of liturgical leadership skills are necessary. The nonchalance and underinvestment of many Protestant pastors in their preaching and worship responsibilities is understandable, given the muddled images of ministry they have been receiving lately, but it is also tragic. Congregational expectations for pastoral performance, particularly in the small church, are invariably tied to the ability to preach, lead worship, and demonstrate a warm, caring attitude in the leadership of Sunday morning activities. Other pastoral activities may be valuable, and even necessary. But the people have the good sense to know that, if a pastor is not helpful in leading them to God in preaching and worship on Sunday, that pastor will not be fundamentally helpful in other church activities that require a *pastor*—not just an organizational director, a community organizer, a social worker, or a good friend.

Furthermore, small churches need to see the Sunday service of their church as their primary activity. For example, most small churches are continually defeated in their attempts to provide the closely graded, elaborately organized programs in Christian education that denominational educators and curriculum resource producers regard as necessary. What can we do about our Sunday school? or How can we have a full youth program? are perennial questions. Many small-church pastors, at a time when they would like to be teaching or supporting the church's Sunday school efforts, are busy rushing from one church to the next between services. We often forget that Sunday school is a fairly recent invention, an innovation of the *laity* who wished to enrich the life of the church. In fact, the case could be made that Sunday school rose in importance at the same rate as investment in, and content and significance of, morning worship declined.

For a very long time, Sunday morning worship served the church as its primary source of education. Here people heard the scripture and listened as it was interpreted with authority and pastoral sensitivity. Here they were not only taught about, but also walked through, the great events and themes of the faith. Rather than lament certain kinds of educational experiences the small church is unable to supply, the pastor should ask, How can I plan and conduct our worship so as to help my people learn more about and grow more firmly into the faith? Teaching sermons are most appropriate on some occasions; the pastor can function as resident Christian educator in elucidating the mysteries of the faith. Children and youth can be involved in the service as Bible bearers, acolytes, ushers, scripture readers, and prayer writers, as a way of teaching them, while they help the whole congregation to worship. In the next chapters we will note the need and the means for restoring more biblical and theological content to preaching and worship, in order to provide people with enough nourishment for growth, within the Sunday service.

The small-church pastor is wise to look for opportunities within Sunday worship for pastoral care, Christian education, motivation for social action, the fostering of community, and the conversion and nurture of the young. For the pastor is probably correct in assuming that if such things do not happen there, as far as the small church is concerned, they will not happen. Congregational worship is a reliable barometer of the life of the small church. Here the church family will celebrate its victories, lament its defeats, act out its deepest needs.

The small church will often express an intense sense of ownership of its Sunday worship practices. It will often resist change in its worship and express anger when its accustomed pattern is disrupted. This resistance and anger are testimony to the importance of the Sunday experience in the life of the small church and should therefore be regarded as positive qualities to be affirmed and enriched, rather than as negative characteristics to be overcome by pastoral manipulation.

The centrality of Sunday worship and its function as the expression and formation of the family's sense of identity is one of the main reasons the clustering, yoking, or team ministry approaches, when they combine the worship services of two or more small churches, are rarely workable. The motives given for those attempts are understandable: the desire for the sense of a larger parish, sparsely attended worship services, and economic problems, as well as the concern for a pastor's time and energy. But the usual outcome of such action is also understandable: further decline in membership, a failure to achieve any real sense of unity or corporate identity, and lack of participation in worship. Each group, if it has any worthwhile function or sense of mission, has a distinct identity, a particular personality. To merge that personality with another, is to destroy both. The motivation to merge the worship services of two small churches usually comes from allowing program or organizational maintenance values to outweigh liturgical and theological values. We can understand why pastors and denominational officials want to combine the services of small churches. We can also understand why the members of small churches resist it.

For nearly two thousand years, pastors administered pastoral care, trained and educated, nurtured and supported, counseled and advised, equipped for social action, and passed on the faith to the young, accomplishing all this by preaching and leading the congregation in corporate worship on Sunday. For most small churches and their pastors today, Sunday is still the basic and most promising asset of their life together.

Chapter Four
The Service of Worship

The bulletin of the full-program suburban church is mailed to each member every Thursday. It contains, in addition to the order of worship for the Sunday service, a list of all the activities for the coming week. The schedule for a typical week in early autumn included:

Sunday: Junior Youth Fellowship roller-skating party
Senior Youth Fellowship cookout

Monday: Women's workshop for annual bazaar
Administrative Council meeting
Basketball game with Trinity Church

Tuesday: Brownie Scouts
Cub Scouts
Finance Committee meeting
Mission study on African independence movements

Wednesday: Mothers' Morning Out baby-sitting program
Social Concern Committee forum on the route of the proposed east/west expressway

Thursday: Cherub Choir rehearsal
Junior Choir rehearsal
Youth Choir rehearsal
Handbell Choir rehearsal
Chancel Choir rehearsal

Friday: Boy Scouts
Young Adult square dance
Fellowship Class potluck dinner

Saturday: Senior Youth Fellowship car wash.

It is difficult, amidst a society of doers, producers, and consumers, to remember that the church is first called to *be*, rather than to *do*. It is so much easier to *do* things. However, God is always the primary actor; we are the recipients of God's loving actions. We have been called by God to be his people, to *join in* God's work—not to *take over* God's work. The "program" of the church is God's, not ours. The church is tempted to regard its efforts as ends in themselves, as if our purpose were more activities carried out by more people, rather than the "increase of the love of God and neighbor"; as if we were to perceive the Christian life as obligation, rather than as response. When we succumb to this temptation, we begin to think that individual Christians exist to support the activities of the congregation and its minister and that the congregation exists to support the activities of the denomination, which does God's work. Ministry is invariably "out there" or "up there," rather than within the scope of the congregation. Church members tend to see themselves as part of a big organization, in which the job of the individual believer is to provide support, funds, and prayers for those

48

somewhere up at the top who do God's work. Theological concerns are constantly in danger of being consumed by denominational concerns.

After reviewing the various purposes of the church's ministry in *Ministry to Word and Sacraments,* Roman Catholic scholar Bernard Cooke concludes by saying, "Yet one cannot avoid the impression that the principal ministry of the community is exercised by *being,* precisely by being a community of faith and love, and as such, bearing witness to the presence of God's saving action in Christ and the Spirit." Once again, the principal business of the church is to *be,* rather than simply to *do!*

But the pastors' actions in the pulpit and at the table during Sunday morning worship should challenge the essentially secular and bureaucratic image of the church and drive it back to its basically theological origins. The small-membership church, which is often the victim, rather than the beneficiary, of the organization and its imperialistic claims, and which can boast few programs other than its Sunday morning program of proclamation and praise, is now in a position to call some of its larger counterparts to return to their theological roots and responsibilities.

The Centrality of Worship

When we worship, we are busy serving God. That is one reason we often refer to the Sunday gathering as a Service of Worship. Worship is the work of Christians. Of course, that work is done both inside church buildings and outside the church. The word "liturgy" means literally, "the work of the people." Whenever the people of God do work that is dedicated to God and responds to the glory of God, that is their liturgy—their worship. Whether it be the liturgy

49

we perform on Sunday or the liturgy we perform Monday through Saturday, it is all of the same piece, all part of our vocation to "glorify God and enjoy him forever." In the New Testament and in the early church, the liturgy of Sunday is indistinguishable from the work of the other days of the week. We serve God by praying to God, singing to God, speaking God's truth in love, feeding the hungry, fighting on God's side, loving the poor, and standing with the oppressed—but it is all worship.

The service of worship on Sunday is central, essential, and primary to all other service to God. As noted in the last chapter, worship is not an optional action among other worthy actions. The woman who says, "I serve the church by working in the Meals for the Elderly program and by helping with the church youth program. I don't see why I need to be in church every Sunday; I don't feel the need to worship," is a person who somehow has misunderstood. Sunday helps to remind us who we are, who we are not, and who, by God's grace, we are becoming. Worship reminds us why we serve and Whom we serve. Sunday is both the motivation for all our service and the judgment upon our service. It reminds us that our activities are not all God's activities. It reminds us that some of our service to the world is done for self-gratification, or merely to give the world what it thinks it wants. Sunday reminds us that the claim upon us is a theological mandate and not merely an altruistic or humanistic attempt to do good deeds. When our spirit weakens and our vision blurs; when the little church becomes overwhelmed with the magnitude of her task and with her failure to be what God has called her to be, Sunday worship restores that hope which will not let us go. How many times, in the life of the small church, has the family gathered—despondent, overwhelmed, hopeless, and confused—only to leave worship as new people? How many times has a fragmented, bickering, weak group of isolated individuals gathered for worship, only to emerge from that hour as the unified body of Christ? In other words, one of the unusual aspects of worship is that, even as we are busy serving God, God is also busy serving us!

In the Southeast, the people in small rural churches sometimes still refer to Sunday worship as "going to meeting." They are speaking as Israel spoke when she named her wilderness sanctuary a tabernacle ("tent of meeting"). In recent years there has been a tendency to look upon Sunday worship as therapy, motivation for social action, an aid to fellowship, a stimulus for individual meditation, or an artistic performance. All these things may occur in worship, but when they are the *purpose* of worship, then what we are engaged in is not Christian worship. In worship, we meet and are met by God, as well as by the people of God. All worship worthy of the name must be an occasion for such meeting.

In our daily life and on Sunday morning, our meetings tend to be accompanied and facilitated by a number of rituals. When we meet a stranger on the street, we have a series of ritualized actions that help us overcome our boundaries and reach out. A handshake, a kiss, a simple How do you do? are all ritualized ways in which we meet each other. Parents instruct their children on the proper way to meet and to be met by others. Without these rituals, our lives might be isolated, self-contained, introverted. The church also has a series of patterned, predictable, ritualized ways to facilitate our meetings with God. An order of worship on Sunday morning is simply a series of ritualized acts, through which we hope to meet and to be met by God.

51

The Bible contains testimony to God's meetings with humanity down through the ages, as well as an affirmation that God will continue to keep his appointed meetings with his people today. Isaiah's meeting with God in the temple; Moses' meeting in the wilderness; Jesus' meetings in the house of Simon and in the upper room, where the meetings were also meals; the meeting in Acts, which became the occasion for the descent of the Spirit and the birth of the church—all suggest occasions, patterns, and results of our meetings with God.

It is not our purpose here to discuss the relative merits of various orders of worship. A congregation's selection of an order of worship for Sunday morning, whether that order is printed in a bulletin, read out of a book, or looked upon simply as the informal leading of the Spirit, is something that should be indicative of that congregation's particular understanding and witness to the faith, as well as of their relationship to the historic liturgical expressions. Too many small churches have been victims of arbitrary worship patterns imposed upon them by their pastors, without regard to the particular nature of those congregations. When the pattern is derived from a large church model of "the right way to worship," the results can be disastrous. An "anthem" performed by a duet of struggling volunteers; a "processional" with a three-member choir, down a twenty-foot aisle; a minister who strikes an aloof and distant stance as if he or she were leading three thousand people, rather than thirty; a little congregation of mostly nonliterate people who spend most of the service thumbing through printed bulletins and the pages of worship books—all show a basic insensitivity and lack of creativity on the part of a worship leader whose models are too limited to be of help to the small-membership church. The response of a congregation to the careless imposition of foreign liturgical styles and patterns may be frustration when they cannot perform them as well as larger churches, rigid resistance (a statement that their former worship pattern had meaning for them), or quiet withdrawal from worship into their own individual meditation or into some worship experience outside the corporate service. The pastor who complains, "My people are not really involved in worship," is often dealing with the end result of thoughtless worship innovation. The people are uninvolved because it is not *their* worship.

This is not to imply that whatever a congregation is accustomed to in its service of worship is always adequate. The worship practices of many small churches are woefully inadequate because of a lack of pastoral attention, or infrequency of worship due to sharing pastors with other churches, or inadequate pastoral leadership from untrained or student pastors, or the disturbing tendency of many small churches to model their services on large-church practices. Therefore, a major order of business in most small churches is to take a careful, critical look at the order of worship, asking, How can we improve our service so that it better expresses who we are, as the family of God and who God is, as the one who has called us together in this place? The question for the pastor of the small church is not, How can I change this congregation's worship pattern so that it fits the denomination's model, or is historically respectable, or is aesthetically pleasing? The question should be, How can I use my pastoral expertise and knowledge of the historic liturgical expressions, to enable my congregation's worship to better form and express their faith?

53

Current Problems in Worship

In observing the Sunday worship services of many small churches, we have observed some major problems.

1. We agree with Helmut Thielicke that the first and foremost purpose of the liturgy is to allow the assembled congregation to be the acting subject of the service of worship and accordingly, to allow it to participate in worship. However, some of our practices seem to foster the people's disengagement from worship, rather than their sharing in it. It is disturbing to see a small-membership church where there is much involvement in all areas of church life, a high level of participation in church meetings, financial support, and welfare ministries, but where the congregation's job at Sunday worship appears to be to sit quietly and watch the pastor perform.

Why is the pastor doing all the scripture reading, praying, announcing, and proclaiming? There is justification for looking on such acts as the sermon, the eucharistic prayer of thanksgiving, the words of forgiveness or pardon, and the benediction as specifically pastoral activities. But the laity can play a much more active role in the service. There are lay people in many small churches who already have had experience in leading worship when a pastor was not present, or on Sundays when they shared a pastor with another church. This lay leadership should be claimed, affirmed, and trained, as a sign of the shared ministry of all Christians within worship.

The use of a printed worship program or bulletin is a fairly recent innovation in Christian worship; the invention of the mimeograph machine made the printed bulletin possible. But this has been a mixed blessing. The only justification for its use is to facilitate the involvement of all the people in the service. If the content of the service or the order of worship never changes, then there is no need for a bulletin. In fact, it is our observation that a bulletin is more often a hindrance than a help to corporate worship. It easily becomes a distraction that enslaves the worshipers to the printed page, with each person's eyes glued to the bulletin rather than fixed upon the leaders and the activities of worship. Protestant worship is already too verbal, too tied to the printed page, too rational and passive, without the use of more printed matter. If one is leading hundreds of people who have never met together and who do not know what to do, then a printed order of worship can be helpful in facilitating their participation. But a family, which lives by a sense of community, order, predictability, informality, and hospitality, has little need of such artificial aids. Unfortunately, a printed bulletin's main use in the small church often seems to be as a status symbol, indicating its desire to resemble a large church.

We would urge pastors to consider the time-honored practice of "bidding" the service—unobtrusively announcing the hymns and the page numbers of prayers and responsive readings. Bidding the congregation through the service reinforces the concept of the pastor as the prompter, guide, and host at worship, rather than as a leader who plods through Sunday activities, with the congregation dutifully following in their bulletins. Where a pastor is serving two or more small churches, a bulletin is probably even more inappropriate, especially if the same one is being used for all the churches. Each congregation needs to feel that, while it is adhering to a widely accepted pattern of worship, its own identity and distinct needs as a congregation are being honored.

Part of the power of the Sunday liturgy is its

predictability, its sameness; there is no need to think about what one is supposed to do next, so that one is free to lose oneself in this ritual of meeting. There is much to be said for choosing a basic pattern of worship and then following that pattern with unvarying regularity until the pastor and congregation are comfortable with it. While the content of each act of worship may be varied each Sunday—in accordance with the church year, the needs of the congregation, the scripture lessons for the day, or some other variable—the pattern itself should be adhered to as a source of stability and structure. For instance, an opening prayer may begin the service every Sunday. But that prayer may be a prayer of confession during Lent, a prayer of thanksgiving during the Easter season, an invocation given by the minister, or a collect led by a lay person. Familiarity with a basic pattern for worship, with seasonal variations in the content, helps worshipers feel comfortable in the service—expectant and involved—while at the same time providing opportunity for the informality and adaptability that make worship in the small church a unique experience. It is the gathering of a family that our order of worship should facilitate—a gathering where each family member feels welcomed and invited to participate—not a carefully orchestrated pageant in which the congregation is primarily the audience, rather than the cast.

2. The basic theological content of our worship needs to be enriched. Those of us who are heirs to the American revivalist tradition often find ourselves in churches where worship is conducted as if the people were in church for the first time in their lives. A kind of warmed-over, yet tragically dissipated, emotional fervor seems to be the goal of the service. The purpose appears to be the fostering of warm feelings, or guilty feelings, or happy feelings, but

not the offering of solid nourishment for spiritual growth. There is too little for the congregation to do in the service; too few theological themes are lifted up in the prayers, readings, hymns, and preaching; and above all, there is a totally inadequate treatment of scripture.

The use of one of the new three-year lectionaries (see Suggestions for Further Reading) to insure a broader treatment of scripture from *both* Testaments; the use of a full order of worship, with ample opportunity for lay participation, in a wide variety of worship words and actions; and careful attention by the pastor to the content of pastoral prayers, the sermon, the seasons of the church year, and the various verbal and nonverbal acts of worship, all will help to insure that people receive the nourishment they need, and the challenge they deserve, from a full celebration and a proclamation of the full gospel.

3. The use of music tends to be either one of the very strong points or one of the weakest aspects of small-church worship. Some small churches sing with an enthusiasm all too rare in a church which once spread across an entire continent on the power of its singing. But in too many small churches, the doleful laments of an inadequate little choir and a woefully limited range of congregational hymns, halfheartedly sung to the poor accompaniment of an untrained musician on a cheap electric organ, tell the story of the sad state of music within small churches. In our discussions with pastors, music tended to be the most frequently mentioned source of irritation on Sunday morning.

Once again, part of the problem is the tendency of the small church to see the larger church as the norm. The history of Christian worship reveals that the choir has often been detrimental to liturgical music. From the medieval *schola cantorum* to the bombastic hundred-voice choirs of American Protestantism, they have a way of robbing the congregation, until the music of worship is reduced to an artistic performance, rather than the song of all God's people. The pastor of the small-membership church should remember that there is something worse than not having a choir on Sunday morning. That something is to have a choir that forgets it is supposed to *aid* the congregation in singing, not do the singing *for* the congregation! One of the most difficult concerns facing contemporary worship renewal is to give the music back to the people. In the small congregation, the people may already bear the burden of music because they have had to do so. In this case, the task is not to build a more impressive choir; it is to enable whatever music leaders a congregation may have to see themselves as leaders and enablers of the congregation, rather than as performers.

One of the main factors in this matter of congregational music is the pastor's own commitment to worship through music. If a pastor enters into congregational singing with enthusiasm, the congregation will often follow that lead. If the pastor enjoys learning (and teaching) new hymns, most congregations will respond in like fashion. While some of the "good old hymns" may be questionable musically and theologically, care must be taken in removing them from a congregation's repertoire. Even the worst of the good old hymns may be better than no hymn at all, since in congregational singing, participation and fervor often compensate for questionable theology. Unfortunately, contemporary hymnody has not given us many singable, theologically adequate hymns to take the place of the old favorites. Whenever new hymns are presented, it must never be in the spirit of, Here is a hymn I like, and you ought to like it, too! but rather, Here is a hymn I think you will enjoy, and that will enrich your own experience of worship!

A Hymn of the Month, sung each Sunday in the month until it is familiar; hymn sings, where the congregation gathers not only to sing the good old hymns, but also to learn a few new ones; and hymns sung by the choir, as anthems, and then taught to the congregation, are all possible ways to "sell" new hymns. A hymn should never be thrust upon a congregation without at least a few minutes of practice singing before the worship service. One church we studied always sings the morning hymns before the service begins, while they await their pastor's arrival from another church. This is not only a good way to gather for worship, but also a good way to brush up on new or unfamiliar hymns. A wider variety of hymns, selected with close attention to the church year, the scripture and sermon for the day, and the overall flow of the service itself, will help to enrich our worship.

The matter of who is to lead or to play for the congregation's singing can be an even greater problem for the small church. Where musical talent may be in short supply, or where dear old Mrs. Jones has led the choir or played the piano for more years than she should, there are no simple solutions. Since music is a deeply personal expression, people tend to be rather sensitive about their own talents and tastes. Pastors are on their own here, and we wish them well! Generally, a good quality piano is superior to a cheap organ; singing *a capella*, or with guitar or autoharp accompaniment, is better than no singing at all. We even found one small church that, without piano or pianist, uses cassette tapes to help its congregation sing.

As in most other small-church dilemmas, the key may be the pastor's own creativity in meeting and solving the problem, not on the basis of what some larger church may be doing, but on the basis of the unique expression of faith in that small church.

4. A few other random difficulties should also be noted so that pastors might consider them as the service of worship is being planned. In many churches there is still a large and inexplicable gap between the time the scripture is read and the time the sermon is preached. A renewed awakening to the joys of biblical preaching suggests that the most logical place for the lessons is immediately before the sermon.

In the service as a whole, there is often a lack of continuity among the lessons, hymns, prayers, psalms, musical offerings, and preaching. This incoherence tends to diffuse the service and send the worshipers off in a dozen different theological and emotional directions at the same time. Better planning and coordination between the pastor and all the leaders of worship is the solution. Generally, we advocate building the service around the theme, or the liturgical context, of the lessons for the day.

In most orders of worship we observed, there is not enough time for, or encouragement of, response to the scripture and the sermon. This does not necessarily mean a formal talk-back session after the sermon, although for some sermons in small churches, this may be a good thing to consider. Sermon talk-back sessions are probably taking place in many small churches already, even if they do not occur in morning worship! But when the sermon is placed at the very end of the worship service, there is not even an opportunity for such responses as an affirmation of faith (Creed), offering, altar call, or prayer. Thus people are given the impression that the Christian faith is nothing more than listening to a sermon and then going home to lunch. Response and responsibility are integral aspects of the gospel. The lessons and the sermon must come early enough in the service so that most of our singing, praying, giving, baptizing, and eating and drinking are seen as responses to the Word, rather than as mere preliminary warm-ups for a sermonic performance.

5. Finally, while we are on the matter of response, we should note that perhaps the most glaring inadequacy in the worship of small churches (as well as of large ones) is the tragic neglect of the sacraments. A major reason that much Protestant worship is weak in theological content and biblical proclamation, provides inadequate opportunity for meaningful congregational involvement, and is too verbal, didactic, rational, and passive, is that the sacraments are no longer a frequent part of Sunday worship. This development is tragic in large churches, but doubly so in small congregations. But this is a larger problem, as well as a source of greater possibility, and we will treat it in more detail in the next two chapters.

Shortly before his death, the great theologian Paul Tillich remarked that, whereas the church of the first part of the twentieth century had to deal with the central issues of guilt and reconciliation, the church of the last half of this century will be forced to deal with the issues of modern humanity's search for meaning and for community. On Sunday morning, as the small church moves through its various acts of worship, it is making a theological statement to itself and to the world about its understanding of the meaning of the life to which God calls us. The church will therefore need to reflect upon its service of

61

worship, to insure that the meaning we express and form in this ritual of meeting is the meaning we intend to express, and that it is being expressed and formed in the best way possible. Worship is also an instrument through which our community is formed as we commune with God. As we meet God, we also meet one another. The church will also need to reflect, to be sure that the community we form in this ritual of meeting is the community God calls us to be—to insure that this community is *God's* community, which exists only to serve by "glorifying God and enjoying him forever."

Chapter Five

The Lord's Supper: Mealtime in the Family

As Jesus moved toward the culmination of his earthly ministry, he gathered his disciples in the upper room of a home and shared a meal with them. How typical of Jesus to take one of the most common and most basic of human acts, a simple meal shared with friends, and transform it into a sacred symbol of God's gift for the world through him.

That meal in the upper room was not to be the *last* supper, for the Gospels describe a succession of meals with the Risen Christ after that sombre Maundy Thursday meal. There was the supper at Emmaus, where the presence of Christ opened the dull eyes of his despondent disciples "when he was at table with them" and when he "opened . . . the scriptures" to them (Luke 24:13-35); that breakfast on the beach where Peter, the "rock" upon which the church was to be built, was commissioned to "feed my sheep" (John 21:17*b*); even that wild, raucous birthday of the church at Pentecost, where the promised descent of the Holy Spirit enabled the transcending of barriers and culminated in the "breaking of bread and prayers" with "glad and generous hearts" (Acts 2:42, 46). Nor was this the end of the mealtime story. From Pentecost forward, when the early church gathered on the Lord's Day, it was for the sharing of what Paul calls the "Lord's supper" (I Cor. 11:20). Eating together, in the name and in the presence of Christ, had become the Christian Sunday thing to do.

Example of the Early Church

Note the words of Justin, written in his *Apology* (I, 67), as he describes the Sunday service of his small church at Rome, about A.D. 150.

> On the day which is called Sunday, all who live in the cities or in the countryside gather together in one place. And the memoirs of the apostles or the writings of the prophets are read as long as there is time. Then, when the reader has finished, the president, in a discourse, admonishes and invites the people to practice these examples of virtue. Then we all stand up together and offer prayers. And, as we mentioned before, when we have finished the prayer, bread is presented, and wine with water; the president likewise offers up prayers and thanksgivings according to his ability, and the people assent by saying, Amen. The elements which have been "eucharistized" are distributed and received by each one; and they are sent to the absent by the deacons. Those who are prosperous, if they wish, contribute what each one deems appropriate; and the collection is deposited with the president; and he takes care of the orphans and widows, and those who are needy because of sickness or other cause, and the captives, and the strangers who sojourn amongst us—in brief, he is the curate of all who are in need. (Bard Thompson, ed. *Liturgies of the Western Church* [Cleveland: World; Meridian Books, 1962].)

What Justin describes is a joyful common meal, a eucharistic act (from *eucharistein,* "to give thanks"), in which the family of God gathers to celebrate, receive, and pass on, the gifts of God.

Today, when the small church gathers on Sunday and celebrates the Lord's Supper (or Holy Communion, or Eucharist), it is very close to the most ancient, most normative, most universal expression of the Christian faith: the small, family-like gathering of Christians around the Lord's Table on the Lord's Day.

In thinking about the celebration of the Lord's Supper within the small-membership church, two things should be kept in mind. First, both Protestant and Roman Catholic liturgical studies of the past few years have focused upon worship in the early church—the first three hundred years of the church, the church that Justin describes—finding the liturgical practices, theology, and ritual of this period to be especially helpful in moving us beyond some of the unfortunate, unproductive, and misinformed dilemmas of past arguments. Many of our inherited rituals and sacramental theologies have been judged inadequate, unbiblical, and limited to the narrow liturgical under-standings of the late medieval Roman Catholic Church or the one-sided perspective of post-Reformation polemic. By jumping over some of our battles of the past four hundred years and looking again at the celebrations of the first years of the church, we have come to some fresh understandings of the Eucharist, understandings which should not be overlooked by small-church worship leaders. Modern liturgical revision has taken its lead from those early Christians. The new eucharistic services among Episcopalians, Lutherans, Roman Catholics, and United Methodists, to mention a few groups who recently have produced new liturgies, are heavily influenced by patristic sources. Simply stated, these new services illustrate that contemporary liturgical renewal is taking its cue from the period before the church became big, successful, and respectable; before the church's worship had a chance to become pompous, dramatic, and extravagant; before the Sunday service degenerated into a preacher/choir performance for a gathering of isolated, passive individuals. Directives for contemporary worship renewal are coming from a church that was then still a family, gathered around a family table, eating a family meal.

Second, in thinking about the Lord's Supper in small churches, we must keep before us constantly an awareness of the particular nature, the strengths and weaknesses, the goals and needs of the small-membership church. While the eucharistic practices of some small churches have suffered because they have been the victims of poorly trained pastoral leadership—part-time student pastors who were not yet authorized to administer the sacraments, or pastors who were shared with a number of churches every Sunday and who viewed the Eucharist as a bother not worth the extra effort—the majority of small churches have innate characteristics making them prime candidates for eucharistic renewal. Most small churches have obvious shortcomings as "organizations," but nearly every small church is a believable family. They like family-type activities. They react to situations as a family would react. A high premium is put upon fellowship, togetherness, and unity, even if, as in any family, such values are often goals, rather than realities. An empty pew at worship has much the same significance as an empty chair at the dinner table. The family feels incomplete. The rhythm of life within a small church is often punctuated by a series of celebrations—festive, important occasions, through which the church family marks off significant points in its life together and confirms its common identity. Invariably, these family-like celebrations are related to meals. Have you ever stopped to think how often, and with what obvious implication, a strong small church eats together? This quality must not be missed as we consider the Lord's Supper in the small church.

Central Themes for Celebrating the Lord's Supper

In recent study of the history, theology and practice of the Lord's Supper, four central themes have emerged. These themes have received amazingly broad endorsement among both Protestant and Roman Catholic scholars, and are relevant to the celebration of the Lord's Supper in small-membership churches.

1. A full service of Word and Table is the norm for Sunday morning worship. A recovery of the Lord's Supper as a frequently celebrated highlight of the church's worship is imperative.

2. The Lord's Supper should focus upon the whole saving work of Christ—his birth, life, passion, death, resurrection, ascension, and present reign—and not simply attempt to reenact the somber meal in the upper room. The Lord's Supper is not a funereal memorial service for a dead friend; it is a joyous victory celebration for a resurrected and reigning Lord!

3. The Lord's Supper is a sign of the unity of the church as the body of Christ. The joy of communal fellowship with Christ and with one another is its goal, rather than individualistic, self-centered, heavily penitential introspection. Sunday is a community and communion day; private meetings with God may take place on other days.

4. At the heart of the Lord's Supper is a meal. Recovery of the meal, where real bread and wine are offered, blessed, and given in sufficient quantities, will

help to reopen the rich symbolism of eating and drinking in the name of Christ.

Having laid out these basic principles regarding the Lord's Supper, we must now suggest some of the practical implications of these principles within a congregation's worship.

First, most of us Protestants need to work at restoring the Eucharist to its rightful place of prominence in the worship life of the congregation. Quarterly celebrations are totally inadequate. In worship, infrequency usually breeds indifference and misunderstanding. Far from making Communion "something special" as some claim, infrequent celebrations usually lead a congregation to regard it as something weird, unusual, optional, tacked on, and completely dispensable. Biblically, historically, and theologically, Christian gatherings on Sunday *without* the Eucharist are unusual.

Protestant Reformers such as Calvin and Luther knew that Word and Sacrament belong together. The prayer, scripture reading, and preaching constitute the proclamation of the faith; the offering, blessing, breaking, and giving of the Communion constitute the enactment of the faith. The Word must not only be preached; it must also be practiced. The Word comes to us not only as words but also as acted-out, tangible, visible symbols. Our words make worship relevant, contemporary, and particular; the Sacraments make worship eternal, transcendent, and universal, uniting us with all those who "at all times and places" have offered themselves and their gifts to God and have in turn seen themselves and their gifts transformed by God.

In churches where the Lord's Supper has been neglected, long-term reeducation may be needed before the congregations are comfortable with more frequent celebrations. The single best way to do this reeducation is through well-planned, enthusiastically led, frequent celebrations. If the sacrament has meaning, it should be self-evident to the participants. One reason the meanings within the sacrament of the Lord's Supper may not be evident, is that we have celebrated it so poorly. Everybody knows what it means to eat together, so the meaning of eating together in the presence of Christ should be obvious. However, if we celebrate the Eucharist in such a way that it is evident to no one that we are at a joyous communal meal, then we already have defeated its significance. Congregations, particularly small congregations, have a way of becoming enthusiastic about whatever their pastor is enthusiastic about (if they are certain that the pastor is *their* pastor). Perhaps they are happy simply to have a pastor who is enthusiastic (literally "filled with the spirit") over anything, or who has any vision of the way things ought to be! If a pastor approaches the Eucharist with the attitude of, "Well, this is all a nuisance but we need to do it anyway," resistance, boredom, and disinterest are sure to infect the congregation as it comes to the table. But if the pastor conveys the attitude that, "This is a special time for me, an occasion for which I have eagerly waited—a rare moment to be with all of you in a very special and intimate way," it takes a dull congregation not to respond in like fashion. Never forget that pastors are educating each time they lead worship. In fact, for the small church, worship may be (as it always should have been for the church) the primary educational event. Pastors must take care when they lead worship, that they teach the things they really mean to teach!

As with any worship innovation, sometimes it helps to

introduce a new attitude toward the Eucharist at a special service, when the congregation is expecting something a bit different and unusual and will be more tolerant of change. Many pastors report that they are able to "sell" their congregation on such new (but actually very ancient) worship practices as the Peace or the common cup by introducing these practices at a Christmas Eve Communion service or on Easter Sunday. While a pastor has the obligation to respect the wishes and feelings of all the members, there is no need to achieve unanimity of opinion, but only a kind of qualified consensus, before introducing new worship practices. Sometimes people do not really know what they like or do not like until they have experienced it over a period of time. One pastor reported that, when his administrative board was reluctant to institute monthly celebrations of the Lord's Supper, he persuaded them to agree to try it for a period of six months, after which time the practice would be evaluated. When the evaluation period came around and the pastor asked the board members for their reaction, he was amazed to hear them respond, "We have always had monthly Communions at this church. It is a tradition here."

In developing pastoral strategies for the recovery of the Eucharist, it helps to discuss the matter with parishioners and to uncover their reasons for resistance to more frequent celebrations. Here are some of the more frequently heard objections.

1. "It takes too long." There is no excuse for long, protracted services. The remedy is mainly a matter of simple mechanics. While the length of the service tends to be less of a problem in the small church than in the large, worship planners must take care that the serving of the

elements is as efficient and yet as unhurried, as possible. Communicants need not be rushed, nor need they be marched back and forth with military precision. This is a meal, not an armed forces parade. The elimination of repetitious "table dismissals," which unduly lengthen and break up the flow of the service, the use of a common cup, and the practice of continuous communion, in which people go to and from the table at their own discretion, will shorten the actual time, as well as enhance the flowing, communal quality of the rite.

2. "I like a full sermon, and on Communion Sundays our pastor usually preaches a little homily, if anything at all." The sermon should never be eliminated from the Eucharist. The preached Word has an integral relationship to the Table. Many Protestants object to more frequent communions because they have the sneaking suspicion that their minister uses these times to take a vacation from preaching. The Lord's Supper offers an excellent opportunity for concrete, lively, contextual sermons. Preaching within the context of the Communion offers an excellent opportunity for pastoral teaching about the meaning of this sacrament. While the sermon may and usually should be short, it must nevertheless be a full sermon. In the context of the gracious, pastoral qualities of this meal, the preacher is free to do his or her most "prophetic" preaching, for the Lord's Supper reminds the congregation that the one who may judge from the pulpit is also the one who feeds and is fed at the Table. As the pastor moves from Pulpit to Table, the people remember that we are *all* hungry sinners, that *all* of us are dependent on the grace that is available here.

3. "It all just seems so sad and sorrowful; I like the joy of our other services. Let's save Communion for Maundy

Thursday." One major reason people often avoid Communion Sundays is that they intuitively suspect that our usually funereal Communions are not consistent with the gospel. Doleful hymns, penitential prayers, people on their knees, somber organ music in the background, sad and "uptight" worshipers, do not seem to have any resemblance to Good News. As we said earlier, the Lord's Supper is *not* simply a repetition of the last supper. We are here to celebrate the whole saving work of God in Christ—not just his passion and death. Many of our inherited rituals for the Communion are unbiblical and theologically limited in their almost exclusive focus upon Christ's passion and death, without reference to his resurrection and reign. We often go forward to the table as if our best friend had died. The Gospels say that our best friend has not died; he is present in our midst! Joyful music should be played, cheerful hymns sung, and bright and festive colors should be in evidence. (One should not only observe a party, but participate in it.) The use of one of the new eucharistic services, the practice of standing for prayer and Communion, and the encouragement of joyous and relaxed participation by all present (militaristic ushers must be taught how to invite people to dinner graciously) will go far in recovering a sense of the Eucharist as true *thanksgiving* and the Lord's Supper as a true meal with a risen and triumphant Lord. A good way to judge the adequacy of the tone and content of your church's celebrations is to ask, "Would our Communion be an appropriate service of worship for Easter Sunday, Pentecost Sunday, or Christmas Day?" If not, your church needs to take care to make its Eucharists truly "eucharistic."

As we said earlier, part of the joy of recovering the Eucharist is the joy of recapturing the centrality of communal fellowship with Christ, and with one another in the body of Christ. Paul stressed this aspect of the Lord's Supper when he told that broken and factionalized church at Corinth, "When you meet together, it is not the Lord's supper that you eat," for they did not discern "the body" (I Cor. 11:20, 29). "The body," in this case, refers to the body of believers that is gathered around the Table. Private, introspective, self-centered worship is out of place on Sunday, because Sunday is a day for us to celebrate life in the body, together. It is a time to come out of our rugged individualism and be transformed into Community, into Family. To paraphrase Paul, "Because there is one loaf, you, many though you are, become one because it is one loaf of which you all partake" (I Cor. 10:17). The very act of eating, whether it be the Lord's Supper or a potluck supper, has a way of bringing us together. For a unified church, the Communion has a way of strengthening that unity. For a divided church, it becomes both an invitation and a means of overcoming disunity. We have noticed on more than one occasion that churches that eat together, like families that eat together, have a way of staying together. Jesus surely knew this when he commanded us to do this often in his name.

Small, individual, communion cups or glasses tend to work against the symbol of a common meal, as well as to fragment the congregation into a conglomeration of self-contained communicants, rather than sustaining it as a unified community. The symbolism of the common cup is self-evident and biblically based. Flat, tasteless, pressed, individual wafers are better symbols of the brokenness of the body of Christ than of either bread or the unity of the body. Such things do make a difference. It must be evident to all that what we are about here is a meal—a meal closely related in significance to all the other meals we eat and therefore implying everything mysterious and profound that every meal implies. But it is also a meal of special meaning, because it is eaten by the community of faith, in the context of our story and our life together, in the setting of our common needs and values, and in the presence of our Lord and Savior. To all who see us, it must be evident that a family, and not just a group of isolated individuals, is gathering here. If celebrated in this fashion, few members of a small church will need their pastor to explain why this meal is central to our faith.

The motivation for recovering more frequent celebrations of the full service of Word and Table is essentially a pastoral one. While there are good and indisputable biblical, historical, and theological reasons for this recovery, the best reason is the pastoral desire to enrich the worship life of the people. Pastors dare to change the accustomed worship patterns (an act which must be done with the greatest of care and sensitivity) out of their conviction that their congregations will be blessed from such change. All other motivation for worship innovation is questionable. In working toward more frequent eucharistic celebrations, pastors do so from a conviction that, particularly in the small church, people desire and enjoy the emotion, intimacy, joy, and family-like fellowship that can come from such celebrations. The task of eucharistic recovery is not as difficult as it may seem—especially within the small church. Those people already know how much fun it is to eat together at picnics or potluck suppers; now how much better to affirm and claim the presence of Christ at their feasts. They already know the joy of remembering a common story, reaffirming and celebrating a common identity, being nurtured and fed by a loving pastor, enjoying membership in a family where one is invited, claimed, loved, fed, and sent forth; now how much better to do all this in the name of Christ.

All these qualities contribute to the small church's readiness to recover the Eucharist as the central worship event. Frankly, the difficulty of making the Eucharist "work" in large churches is enormous. Large churches are rarely ready to have true Communion, and table fellowship is often an unusual event. The small church is different. The distance between its potluck suppers in the fellowship hall and its Lord's Suppers in the sanctuary is not so great. It is in such family-like churches that true worship renewal will occur, long before their larger counterparts will taste this fresh new wine.

This chapter opened with an account of small-church worship from the second century; now it closes with an account of small-church worship from the twentieth.

> I attended the Homecoming Sunday at a little rural church served by one of my former students. "Homecoming" at this church involved the return to the church of those who had moved away, the cleaning and care of the church's cemetery, some sort of recognition of those who had died during the past year, and a big covered-dish dinner on the grounds.
>
> Joe, the young pastor, invited a guest preacher, as was the custom. He also suggested to the church board that the Lord's Supper be celebrated during the service. While the church had become accustomed to at least monthly celebrations since Joe had come to the church, some of the board members were hesitant because of the large number of visitors they were expecting, and because they had always been accustomed to "just having a sermon and then going out and eating." After some discussion, Joe

75

got them to agree to give it a try (this was the usual outcome of their discussions—they liked Joe and were usually willing to give his new ideas a fair chance).

For the service, Joe used a new communion service, published by his denomination and designed for use on All Saints' Day or on other days when a church wished to have a service centering around the communion-of-saints theme. It seemed appropriate for a homecoming setting.

The little sanctuary was packed, and an atmosphere of expectancy filled the air. The hymns were joyful, affirmative, and well sung by the larger-than-usual congregation. Most dealt with the themes of the church, its heritage, and its mission. The scripture lesson was Matthew's account of the calling of the disciples. The preacher used this text to reflect upon the duties of discipleship, making reference in his sermon to the heritage we have been given by disciples who have preceded us. It was noted that many different kinds of people, with many different strengths and weaknesses, have gathered at the communion rail in the church and that our gathering today links us with those who have come forward and served in the past.

Immediately after the sermon, the pastor led the people in an intercessory prayer (after they had made a number of requests for special prayers for various needs). At the end of the prayer, the lay leader read aloud the names of the people in the congregation who had died during the past year. A number of people were visibly moved at this point. It was a very emotional moment. The Peace, which immediately preceded the offering, was a perfect expression of the unity and emotion the congregation was now feeling and a fitting prelude to the Table. Many in the congregation not only joined hands but also embraced. The Peace merely expressed, in visible form, what they had felt throughout the service.

As the offering was received, a young couple brought forward the bread and wine. She carried a loaf that was, obviously and delightfully, homemade bread; he bore a large pitcher of wine. The pastor received the offering, poured the wine into a battered and worn, antique, and evidently much-loved chalice.

Then the pastor led the people in a special prayer of thanksgiving, or eucharistic prayer, which focused on the communion-of-saints theme. "Come to the Lord's Table," was his invitation to the Communion. As the people came forward, the little choir led the whole congregation in singing such hymns as "Faith of Our Fathers," "The Church's One Foundation," "Blest Be the Tie That Binds," and other old favorites relating to the theme of the day. People were invited to come forward at their own discretion, to kneel at the communion rail as long as they wished, and to indicate when they wished to receive the elements by holding out their hands. People seemed to appreciate this freedom to come when they wished and to stay as long as they wished.

Even in this relaxed, free method, the fifty or sixty people present were able to partake of the elements within six or eight minutes. The pastor would place a large chunk of bread in each person's hands, look him or her in the eyes and call each by name. "John, the Body of Christ, broken for you." "Mary, the Body of Christ. . . ." He was followed by the lay leader, who administered the cup in a similarly sensitive and caring way. I noted that many people grasped the pastor's hands as he gave them the bread. The relationship between pastor and people was obvious.

As the service ended (in just under an hour), the pastor mentioned that he and the lay leader would be taking Communion to the home of the oldest member of the church that afternoon, and he asked if any other members might need to be visited with Communion. Then the entire congregation stood, sang the doxology, and were blessed by their pastor.

As we were leaving the sanctuary, one elderly woman said to me, "That was the way Communion used to be in this church. We always used to have glad, warm services with lots of feeling. Since Joe has been with us, that's the way they have been again. I'm glad he knows the way we are and lets us be ourselves. Let's eat."

We walked out of the church and toward a grove of oak trees, where the homecoming meal was just about to begin.

Chapter Six

Baptism: The Family Claims Its Own

No one can elect to join a family. One has to be adopted. It is the family that must do the accepting and the electing. In this book we have compared the small church to a family, noting the similarities of the tensions, limitations, and opportunities to those within any family. One reason newcomers to the small church sometimes receive the impression that the church is closed, cold, exclusive, and reluctant to open itself up to new members, is that the small church behaves as a family does. A person cannot "join" a family by deciding to join and signing a membership card as if one were joining an organization; one must be adopted. One of the dangers of attempting to become a member of a small church is that one may be a victim of its reluctance to adopt newcomers into its family life. One of the joys of becoming a member is the possibility of being adopted and claimed as part of a caring, nurturing, loving family. When small churches "work," the possibility of adoption is a constantly recurring reality. Baptism is part of that adoption process through which the small church claims its own.

In an impersonal, nameless, rootless world, most small churches are expert in the art of helping people to discover where they belong. In the small church, everyone has a name—sometimes even a nickname—a place in the life of the church, his or her own place to sit on Sunday morning, his or her own job to perform. Identity is celebrated, confirmed, and constantly reaffirmed. A new pastor will be carefully instructed on "the kind of people we are here." Violations of, or attempts to change, that identity will be noted and reprimanded. "We're just not like that," the offender will be told.

Related to its familial caring quality is the small church's nurture of its young. When a small church is not blessed with many children and youth, it cares all the more for the few it has. Worship will often be accompanied by the din of little feet and voices as the youngsters squirm and squeal their way through the service. Protesting infants will be passed up and down the pew until someone finds a means of diversion. There is always an adequate number of grandparents so that every young mother has someone to help keep her children reasonably contained. Small churches tend to be disinterested in nursery care during worship services, not simply because there are too few children to make it worth the effort, but also because they want their whole family together, young and old, when they gather to praise God. Children are claimed, loved, watched, disciplined, and cared for, in the small church. And when those children grow up, there is always someone still around who remembers "when I used to have to keep you quiet during church" and who continues to reinforce the growing child's awareness that he or she is one of the family.

All these characteristics are positive attributes when the small church celebrates the identifying and initiating sacrament of the Christian faith—baptism.

In baptism, God acts through water to enlarge the family of God and to redeem its members through their identification with a crucified and risen Lord. Baptism is our adoption by God and by the family of God, our assignment of a place and a task in the kingdom, our naming as God's own, our ordination as members of a "chosen race, a royal priesthood, a holy nation, God's own people, that you may declare the wonderful deeds of him who called you out of darkness into his marvelous light" (I Peter 2:9). The mandate given to God's people is to "make disciples . . . baptizing . . . teaching" (Matt. 28:19, 20). Our mission is to "make disciples" by initiating them into the family through baptism and by continuing to teach those who are now in the family.

While the New Testament tells us almost nothing about *how* we are to baptize (the method), or even the qualifications of *who* we are to baptize (the age, belief, or status of the recipient), it does say much about the rich meanings within baptism: forgiveness of sins, rebirth, purification, death, resurrection, adoption, light. In short, baptism means everything to us that water itself means. Baptism signifies a radical, revolutionary event, through which the risen Christ has "qualified us to share in the inheritance of the saints . . . delivered us from the dominion of darkness and transferred us to the kingdom of his beloved Son, in whom we have redemption, the forgiveness of sins" (Col. 1:12-14). Baptism marks the beginning of a conversion experience that is both death and life; "We were buried therefore with him by baptism into death, so that as Christ was raised from the dead by the glory of the Father, we too might walk in newness of life" (Rom. 6:4).

Requirements for Baptism

In recent studies and in ecumenical discussions of baptism, there has been broad agreement on the necessary preconditions for a full, normative baptism. The three requirements for a baptism in its biblical, historical, and theological dimensions are (1) water; (2) a responding person who is to be baptized; and (3) a believing community to do the baptizing.

First, one must have water. Through an odd series of unfortunate circumstances, the amount of water used in the rite of baptism became less and less. Baptismal fonts went from bathtub- to fingerbowl-size in a few centuries. As the amount of water diminished, our baptismal theology also seemed to decline. Early church writings about baptism as being "death," the "waters of the womb," and "a cleansing bath" make no sense when the water of baptism is reduced to a mere sprinkle. We thereby cut ourselves off from some of the rich biblical imagery formerly associated with the rite. If the things that are done and said in baptism could be done and said in any other way, then we would not have been commanded to do and say them through water. If the amount of water is irrelevant, then why use it at all?

The new baptismal services among Roman Catholics and many Protestants stress the abundant use of water. The question for these services is not, How can we use as little water as possible and still have a valid baptism? The question is, How can we flaunt this effusive grace which God pours upon us in baptism? One reason many people in our churches do not understand the rite of baptism is that they have never participated in a full, robust, bold celebration. In those churches that already have and use a full-sized baptismal pool, the presence and use of water is no problem. In new or renovated churches, we must be sure to build larger, more significant baptismal pools and fonts, placing them in a conspicuous place in the church. Immediately inside the front door is a good place for a font or pool, since this reminds us that baptism is "the door into the faith"—the rite of passage into the Christian family.

If the so-called baptismal font is small and insignificant in your church, it is still possible to have more adequate baptisms by making certain changes in the way they may have been celebrated. For instance, a big pitcher of water can be brought forward by a member of the congregation at the time of the baptism, which should occur sometime after the sermon, but before the Lord's Supper—this underscores baptism as a response to the Word and as an admission to the Table. The minister should then boldly pour the water into a generously sized bowl, making sure everyone sees and hears the flowing water, and should not be afraid even to spill some of it in the process. When the actual baptism is performed, the person being baptized should get wet—convincingly, visibly wet. Obviously, immersion is the best way to show the powerful symbolism of water and its connotation of life, death, birth, resurrection, and purification. Pouring of the water beautifully symbolizes the union of baptism with the gift of the Holy Spirit: "I will pour out my Spirit on all flesh" (Acts 2:17). The widespread sprinkling method utilizes an inadequate amount of water in the rite, obscuring the water's sacramental significance. Throughout the new baptismal rites, there is a renewed emphasis upon the visible, concrete, tangible way in which God imparts his grace to us through the sacraments. The abundant use of water, the giving of a lighted candle—"You are the light of the world" (Matt. 5:14); the dressing of the baptized in a white robe—"Who are these, clothed in white robes . . . ?" (Rev. 7:13); the signation of the forehead of the candidate—"In him you . . . were sealed with the promised Holy Spirit" (Eph. 1:13), are all ways to show forth this mystery we celebrate in baptism.

Second, one must have a responding person. While baptism represents God's *a priori* acceptance of us, and while it is primarily something that God does to and for us through the Christian community, Christian baptism demands a response from the one being baptized. The Apostles' Creed is an early baptismal creed. Baptism signifies that not only have I been adopted, accepted, and initiated into God's family, but also that I have accepted that adoption. The grace is free, unmerited and unearned, but for this very reason, it necessitates response. Some churches baptize only adults, believing that only they are capable of the kind of response baptism demands. Other churches baptize infants of Christian parents, seeing baptism as a continuous, lifelong process of initiation into the faith, which requires a lifetime of responsiveness and growth. Both groups practice "believer's baptism," even though they differ on how and when belief comes about. Both groups see baptism as a sign of God's love and grace, although they view our human response to that grace in somewhat different ways.

It should be noted, however, that the real issue here may not be simply a question of the right age of response. The question may be phrased more accurately as, What is the content, the goal, the meaning of our response? Churches that think they have solved the problems of response in baptism simply by decreeing that no one but adults (the definition of "adult" is often applied rather loosely in many believer's-baptism churches) are as mistaken as those that think they have solved the problem simply by requiring that the child's parents have their names on the church roll. For both churches, the questions are: What is the best way to produce Christians? What kind of church do we want? What is the best way to form that church?

Neither the "adult baptizers" nor the "child baptizers" are relieved of the struggle of seriously considering the way the family is to nurture its members in order that their whole lives may become continual response and responsibility to the God who has named them, claimed them, and loved them, in baptism.

Recent studies have stressed the need for a new acceptance of responsibility on the part of the church in regard to conversion and nurture. The church can no longer assume, if it ever really could, that people will grow up Christian just by living in our society. The church must exercise a new intentionality in its dealings with those whom we initiate into the faith, at whatever age. Baptism is the beginning of the Christian pilgrimage—not the end of it; it is the start of a lifelong process of conversion—not a once-and-for-all event. As Luther is said to have remarked, "Our old sinful selves are drowned in baptism. But the old Adam is a mighty good swimmer." While baptism is a rite that can occur only once, it takes a whole lifetime to finish our conversion.

In reading descriptions of Christian initiation, particularly in the pre-Constantinian period, we are impressed with the serious attitude of the church toward this task. In an age and a surrounding culture strikingly like our own, the early church apparently felt the need to carefully convert, educate, and discipline those who sought entrance into the family of God, as well as to signify publicly, liturgically, and dramatically through baptism, the transition the new Christian was making. The contemporary church has been all too casual in fulfilling its task of making disciples. Catechesis, the task of educating and nurturing people for discipleship, is emerging again as a major part of the church's ministry. For too long, small churches have lamented that they cannot fulfill certain preconceptions of the qualities of Christian education. They often cannot afford denominational literature and cannot meet denominational expectations for closely graded classes, teacher training, and equipment. Too often, Christian education has patterned itself on secular education. This is unfortunate, since, unlike secular educational objectives, the objective of all Christian education should be the making of disciples and not the mere imparting of knowledge. We want not only to nurture people, but also to convert people. We are looking for response—not simply assimilation of facts.

Christian education (whatever the church does to nurture and convert its people into the faith and the demands of discipleship) should be seen as part of the baptismal process. And Christian education and baptism are elements of the process of Christian initiation, which takes one's whole lifetime to bring to completion. Pastors must take their cue from the early church and once again become earnest about prebaptismal instruction. When an infant is to be baptized, they must be sure that the child's parents or other persons in the congregation take personal responsibility for insuring that the child is nurtured into the faith. If there are no suitable sponsors for the child, then there must be no baptism, because when there is no one to respond for the child and to nurture the child's own response, baptism is a mockery. There is no harm in postponing baptism until parents and/or sponsors are better committed and prepared to truly respond for the child, or until the child is mature enough to respond for him- or herself. The small church is an excellent place for the response and nurture that baptism demands. The almost instinctive manner in which it claims and guides its young should be affirmed and enriched, as a specific vocation of any responsible church.

Before youth or adults are baptized, instruction of the candidates by the pastor (assisted by the congregation) is equally important. Retreats, small-group study sessions, evening discussions in the candidates' homes—these are some of the ways a pastor might fulfill the need for prebaptismal instruction and counseling. Even for youth and adults, a sponsor, appointed by the church, can be given the responsibility for personally overseeing the nurture of the new Christian and insuring that this initiate becomes a functioning member of the body of Christ. Pastors must use all the resources at their disposal to remind the people that the Christian faith is more than just sitting and listening; it is also response.

As the Reformers often noted, response in baptism is a continuing process for the Christian. Baptism is the beginning of the Christian pilgrimage, not the end of it. The new baptismal services, in most denominations, provide for periodic opportunities for members of the congregation to renew their vows through various kinds of services. A wise pastor will make frequent use of such worship occasions as Easter, Pentecost, New Year's Day, and Homecoming, for recommitment, renewal, and response. Rites of confirmation, evangelistic altar calls, and other such worship activities, which are part of some churches' traditions, are best interpreted as a means of remembering and reaffirming our baptism. Most people will welcome opportunities to reaffirm their faith. When possible, such renewal should be done within the context of a baptism, reminding the newly baptized of the continuing need for growth and response in faith, and the previously baptized of their need to continue to be remade into God's image for us. Postbaptismal instruction is as important as prebaptismal instruction.

The third requirement for a full baptism is that it be done *within the context of a believing community.* Historically, we have affirmed that baptism is essentially something that God does, through the church. Unfortunately, in our individualistic, self-help, Pelagian society, we have stressed the actions of the one being baptized more than we have stressed the actions of the community doing the baptizing. We have argued about the proper disposition, age, knowledge, or behavior of the prospect, when we should have paid more attention to the disposition and faith of the church that baptizes. Baptism has been called adoption. God adopts us as his children, and the church therefore adopts us as her members. As in any adoption, it is the one who does the adopting, rather than the adoptee, who does most of the accepting, affirming, and acting. In past arguments over the proper age to baptize, polemic often obscured the fact that our focus should be upon the church and the way God works through the church in baptism, rather than upon the recipient. The main burden of faith and action is upon the baptizers. For at whatever age baptism occurs, it is the *church* that bears the responsibility to "make disciples" by baptizing and teaching. This is why baptism should always be celebrated as a prelude to participation in the Lord's Supper. We must move from Font to Table as a visible reminder that baptism is the way into the family and the rite of passage to the family's table. There are no compelling theological reasons to prohibit the communion of baptized infants and children. In fact, to baptize without then admitting the newly baptized to the Table raises serious theological questions about the purpose and function of baptism. The move from Font to Table reminds us that we are now forever dependent upon the family for nurture and nourishment in the faith.

This is the reason baptism must never be (except in the most extreme and unusual of circumstances) a private rite. The presence of a believing community is necessary. New baptismal liturgies give the congregation more overt participation in the baptismal action: the congregation joins in the baptismal confession of faith, lay people present the candidates, and sponsors are recognized. And here we come to one of the most basic problems with baptism in the contemporary church. Too often, the church is in the absurd position of baptizing people into a "community" that is little more than a gathering of strangers who care little about the one being baptized, are unclear about their own faith, and who take little or no responsibility for the care and nurture of anyone except themselves. The real problem with baptism today is not so much with the people we are baptizing, but rather with the community that is doing the baptizing. It is the faith and sincerity of the community that is the problem—not the disposition of the persons being baptized. This is the reason that today, both in churches that practice infant baptism and in those that do not, a new concern is being expressed for the response of the community. Our problem is not so much one of a proper method of baptism, as it is one of a proper manner of being integrated into the church.

In a transient society where the membership of a congregation is always shifting; where there is little carry-over or contact from one generation to the next; where long-term care and nurture is difficult, baptism is problematic. In a large, impersonal church, where few people know or really care about one another, baptism is particularly uncertain. Fortunately, in many small churches, these problems are less severe. The stability, the intergenerational contact, the family-like quality of the small church, all make it well-suited as the context for lifelong baptismal experience. As in our discussion of the Lord's Supper, it is our feeling that baptismal renewal will more than likely first come about within the smaller congregations.

The pastor has responsibility for nurturing the kind of supportive community where the claiming, disciplining, affirming, and making of disciples is possible. The pastor needs to reflect constantly on ways people can grow in the faith, ways those who are still on the fringes can be made to feel more a part of the family, and ways the family can incorporate new life into its midst. If there are those within the family who have been wronged or forgotten; if there are youth and children who are not being properly nurtured; if there are those who seem to be growing away from the family, the pastor needs to note these problems, call them to the attention of the family, and guide its thoughts in better fulfilling its baptismal responsibilities to these members of the body of Christ.

Baptism, at whatever age it occurs, is always a visible, tangible reminder ("God's Word in water," Luther called it) that I am who I am in great part because of those who have loved me, and claimed me, and cared for me. It is a statement that my identity is a corporate product, that I can never be faithful in isolation or in irresponsibility, and that I will find myself only in community with others, and only by responding to others. Baptism is God's reaching out to me through the church, to love me, claim me, change me, remake me, guide me, until I am made over into his image, which he has placed upon me. Baptism is a sacrament of comfort to us in our troubled times, because God is a jealous God who keeps what he owns, and baptism is a declaration that God owns *me*. In baptism, and in continuing baptismal activities, such as Christian education and pastoral care, the small church acts as a family, to name its own, claim its own, look after its own, and identify its own, until those whom the family claims respond as part of the family—the Family of God.

Chapter Seven
Weddings and Funerals:
Crises Within the Family

Life within the small church, like life within a family, is sure to impress the outside observer with its strong sense of ritual—patterned, predictable, repetitive behavior. Every important occasion has its prescribed set of behaviors, its predictable series of events, its given range of expectations. These are the rituals by which the small church confirms its identity and passes down to succeeding generations its sense of place and purpose. Without the rituals, informal and formal, inside the church and out, in Sunday morning worship and at the Wednesday board meeting, there would be no church family.

Ritual is necessary because it is our link with our past, our guidance from previous generations who have been through it all before—our legacy. Also, ritual is needed because it helps to create community, to form consensus, to foster and maintain corporate values and norms. The question before any religious group that strives for more than the creation of a mere conglomeration of isolated, idiosyncratic, religious loners, is not, Shall we live by ritual? (for this is not an option), but rather, Will our rituals adequately express and form our faith?

Rituals perform yet another function for us: they help us cope with stress and anxiety. Nowhere is this function more evident than within those that some have designated "life-crisis" rituals. Throughout our lives, we are forced to move across boundaries from one identity, or state of being, to another. Birth, the first day of school, high school graduation, the first job, the death of a parent, marriage, retirement—these are some of our significant life transitions.

Fortunately, the church has always utilized a complex series of formal and informal rituals to guide us through the most difficult transitions. The more threatening and potentially disruptive the crisis, the more detailed and carefully patterned will be the life-crisis ritual. In this chapter we will focus on two significant crises—the crisis of marriage and the crisis of death—noting how the small church can bring its liturgical resources to bear on the needs of its members at these turning points, in the same way any loving family rallies to support its members in such situations.

Weddings

Weddings are family affairs. In all the hustle and bustle of announcing the date, inviting guests, making plans, and attending to the thousands of small and large details, sometimes one has to search for the bride and groom amidst worried mothers, nervous fathers, officious directors, visiting cousins, adoring aunts, and out-of-town friends. One may ask, Whose wedding is this? And that is exactly the first question that should be asked!

A wedding in a Christian church is a service of worship. As with any such service, a wedding should not be thought of as a private affair. While the love and the vows of this man and woman have occasioned the gathering, and while the church's primary concern is to aid them in their movement from single to married life, the bride and groom are not our only concern. A wedding, like any service of worship, belongs to the church. It is a

93

thoroughly public, corporate affair—and that is its strength. In other words, a wedding is for the whole church family. A wedding not only allows the church to provide its resources (traditions, experience, values, support) for the needs of the bridal couple, but it also provides an occasion to minister to the church family as a whole. The bride and groom are not the only persons who are making a difficult transition. Their parents, friends, and relatives are also having to adjust to a new status and changed relationships.

One of the disturbing tendencies in some current approaches to the wedding is to view it as "only for the bride and groom," to accommodate their tastes in music and their individual understandings of what the marriage service should be. This robs the couple of the rich, historic, intergenerational resources the church has to offer during this time of passage. It also tends to deny parents and friends a meaningful part in the service, since the bride and groom have become sole designers and focus of the ritual. Over half the liturgy of most traditional wedding services is addressed to the congregation as a whole. In so doing, the church seems to be saying to all the rest of us—those who are already married, those who are preparing for future marriage, and those who are having to change our lives because of this particular marriage—that important things must be publicly done and said through this public ritual of union; that the church has something important to say to all of us. The family-like atmosphere, the links across generations, the ties with the past, and the generally high level of participation in a small church, are all positive factors when applied to weddings. Pastors of small churches should look for ways to reinforce the natural tendency of the small church to act as a family acts during life crises. Planning of the wedding should involve the entire church. They should look upon this liturgical event as *their* wedding, needing everyone's resources, talents, and support. At one small church we visited it was customary for the congregation to present the wedding reception to the bride and groom as their wedding gift. The people in the church decorated the fellowship hall and provided the refreshments and music. We were told that the tradition arose when the church realized that some families could not afford to have a full reception, so the church decided to provide a reception as their contribution to each wedding. At another church it is the practice for the lay leader or some other member to give a blessing at each marriage, as a sign of the congregation's presence and support.

Another major implication of our definition of a wedding as a service of worship is that it should be judged by the same standards and criteria by which we judge any service of worship. If the church feels that Christian worship should be corporate, or participatory, or biblically based, or theologically focused, or evangelistic, or missional, or offer any other such essential, then it should demand the same standards of its weddings. Too often a wedding is planned and celebrated in a manner conveying the feeling that the Service of Holy Matrimony is anything *but* worship.

If weddings belong to the church, then the pastor should spend time with some representative group in the church, establishing guidelines and statements about what is expected of weddings in that church. It is unfair for a pastor to arbitrarily set his or her own standards for the content of a marriage service, but it is the pastor's duty to enforce a congregation's established wishes. The day before the wedding is not the appropriate time to argue with the bride regarding music. After a number of unfortunate arguments about music, flowers, and other details, one church we visited determined to make a study and write a Statement of Purpose, along with a set of guidelines, for the planning of weddings within the congregation. After a few weeks of consideration and discussion with the pastor, they decided to expand the inquiry to include all services of worship within the little church. The result was the publication of a booklet entitled *Worship at Red Hill Church*, which discussed all worship events at the church, what the church was trying to do and say during these services, and its standards for each service. These booklets are now given to all who join the church. The congregation has a new sense of ownership of its worship life and a new appreciation of its meaning.

Some questions for consideration by a church that is evaluating its celebrations of Holy Matrimony are: (1) Are weddings within our church full services of worship? (That is, do they include sufficient scripture, congregational participation, a short sermon, creed, hymns, and so forth?) (2) Who is the "director" of our weddings? (3) What is the role and the limitation of special decorations, such as flowers, in services of worship? (4) What about photographs? (5) What is the central symbol and what symbolic actions should be focused upon during a Christian wedding, and how can we keep these symbols from being obscured? (6) What roles could the Sacraments play? (7) How much premarital preparation do we think a couple ought to have with our pastor? (8) How can we more adequately prepare our youth for future marriage, and how can we more adequately support the marriages we already have in this congregational family? (9) What is the policy concerning clergy from other churches? (10) How can we be sensitive to the individual needs and wishes of the bride and groom and still be faithful to the church's historic witness in marriage?

Funerals

Some of the same perspectives and guidelines suggested for marriages within the small church can be applied to funerals. Just as a wedding is the church's liturgical response to the crisis of marital union, so a funeral is the liturgical response to the crisis of death. Few occasions in life require a more intentional, careful, theologically informed response by the church than does death. And few human gatherings are better able to respond to this crisis than the small church.

When death comes, a drastic alteration is precipitated in the existence of those persons who were close to the deceased: relationships are severed; a part of them dies; their lives are thrown into confusion. Grief is the natural expected response to the crisis of death, and the funeral can be a valuable means of working through the grief. In the disorientation, isolation, and pain that often accompany grief, the community's rituals—both the formal rituals of the funeral and the informal rituals before and after the funeral—are important ways to help grieving persons make sense out of the situation and move to a new understanding of themselves in the absence of the person who has died.

In thinking about funerals in the small church, the first need is to list all the rituals—the patterned, predictable behavior—utilized by that church in responding to a death in its congregational family. This is particularly important for new pastors, since all churches tend to have their own series of formal and informal rituals which pastors must learn if they are to be effective leaders of these rituals. Sometimes, the informal rituals that occur outside the church building may be as important as the formal ones, because the informal rituals help prepare people for the funeral liturgy itself.

What happens, almost automatically, when someone dies? The pastor and the funeral director are called, friends and relatives arrive at the home to begin comforting the bereaved and getting the house in order for visitors. Meals are prepared, out-of-town relatives are contacted, a coffin is selected, and funeral arrangements are made. This flurry of activity and this predictable series of events are extremely important parts of the grief process. These activities, no matter how mundane and ordinary they may seem, help us to deal with a mystery most of us are reluctant to approach—death. They give everyone something to do, a way to keep busy, a means of coping with the crisis. The women who prepare food and bring it to the bereft family are not only being helpful to the family; they are also acting out their own need to respond to their friends' crisis. In fact, the helpfulness of the funeral itself may be lessened if a church has not adequately developed the extraliturgical rituals to be put into practice before and after the funeral. It has been our impression that small churches, where everyone knows everyone else; where absent members are missed; where old and young are in frequent contact with one another; where familial-type responsibility is felt, develop and utilize these pre- and postfuneral rituals better than larger churches.

If the pastor has been with the family from the very beginning of the grief process (something that is also easier to do in smaller congregations); if the pastor has had the time to meet visiting relatives and friends and to plan the funeral service with the family, as well as to care for the larger community, which may be going through its own grief over this death, then the pastor is more able to give firm, assured, and reassuring liturgical leadership in the funeral itself. He or she can then make use of the funeral liturgy as *pastoral* care and not simply "go through the service."

The pastor has been given the responsibility for being the "funeral director," functioning in much the same way as at any service of worship. This must be clear from the beginning. What was said about weddings applies also to funerals. These are services of corporate, Christian worship. The pastor's task in leading a funeral is not only to "do whatever the family wishes," but rather, it is to lead the Christian community in its worship, proclaiming the Word, possibly administering the Sacraments, guiding the service on the basis of the church's historic, theological, and biblical response to death. In so doing, the pastor will find that the church family will be cared for and ministered to in a way that is more appropriate for Christian pastoral care than is an irresponsible, misguided attempt to respond only to the wishes of the relatives of the deceased.

As with the wedding, the funeral is for the whole church family. While our first concern is for the persons in the congregation who are going through this acute crisis of grief, the entire family of God is in need of the church's witness at a funeral. A funeral not only ministers to a specific grieving family, it also ministers to those of us who are dealing with unfinished grief from past deaths, as well as those of us who must prepare for future bereavement. The tendency toward small, private, graveside services, limited to a handful of selected close friends and relatives who are led through an abbreviated service, is a disturbing tendency. The small private gathering may not only represent a subtle attempt to avoid the reality of death, but it also may be a denial of the witness and the participation of the entire Christian community at the time of death. Any funeral is for the whole congregational family.

A thorough study of funerals is a worthy task for any congregation. The time to improve funerals, to educate people about funerals, and to set congregational standards, is not on the day of the event. Some churches make a Funeral File, in which all adult members are asked to complete a form, in consultation with the pastor, in which they state their wishes for their funerals. These forms can be a great help to the relatives when death occurs. Having the funeral at the church, with a full service of worship, encouraging full congregational participation and full utilization of the church's music, scripture, prayer, creed, and sacraments, will help to bring the best of its liturgical resources to the crisis of death and bereavement.

In a sometimes impersonal, detached, rootless world, where men and women often relate to one another as "things," to be casually used and thoughtlessly abused, rather than as God's beloved children who are always to be honored and cherished; where death is either avoided, denied, or handled in impersonal mechanized ways which rob both life and death of their God-given dignity, the family of God, particularly when it gathers in the small church, has a Word to proclaim. Careful, informed consideration of its rituals of marriage and death can help the small church proclaim that Word with the clarity, warmth, and care the world so desperately needs.

Chapter Eight
Preaching in the Small Church: Serving the Word

While preaching has remained central in the life of the black church and is now being rediscovered in the Roman Catholic Church, it has fallen upon hard times in most main line white Protestant churches. A score of critics have questioned the effectiveness of preaching, its authoritarian image, or its suitability for a modern television-oriented generation. The pastor who still devotes a major portion of time to the preparation of sermons is a member of a rare breed. Today it is pastoral counseling, routine visitation, parish administration, or community activity that consumes the pastor's time. As Leander Keck says, "Sundry matters have displaced Sunday matters." When many preachers speak this Sunday, the congregations will not have to be told that their pastors set aside little time for reading, reflection, prayer, and other requisites of good sermon preparation. The pastors' own low opinion of the preaching office will be evident in their sermons.

In the next chapter we will examine the not-so-surprising data, confirming that congregations—at least the small congregations we studied—continue to rate preaching at the top of a pastor's various duties. So why do pastors now neglect that duty regarded by their parishioners with such esteem? The factors are many and complex. Some modern criticism has tended to fragment and distort the Bible as a reliable source for sermons. The exegetical methods many preachers learned in seminary reveal all the things that *cannot* be said about a given text, rather than those that *can* be legitimately preached. Some communications theorists have raised questions about the effectiveness of the essentially one-way communication techniques of preaching. Many of the modern ethnic, liberation, *ad hoc*, unsystematic, *avant garde* theologies are not yet well formed enough to lend themselves to the weekly preaching needs of the average congregation. Modern views of the nature and purpose of the church see it as a place for counseling, for administration of an organization, or as a base for social action, rather than as a place for the "due administration of Word and Sacraments." In many of the larger Protestant denominations, clerical advancement is determined more on the basis of faithful service to the parent organization, relationships with other clergy, or performance in denominational projects and parish building programs, rather than on the preaching of the Word within the local congregation.

All these factors coalesce to draw pastors away from heavy investment in preaching. Besides, let us be honest—preaching is difficult: a wide range of exegetical, theological, psychological, and homiletical skills are required for good preaching. Many pastors have not been given, nor have they had the inclination to develop, these skills. For them, the preaching office is better avoided than confronted.

Authority for Preaching

If there are those who charge that contemporary preaching is inadequate, they must have some idea what adequate preaching sounds like. What is "good" Christian preaching? While it is not within the scope of this book to discuss all the aspects of preaching, we are convinced that every pastor of a small church must come to a more adequate understanding of good preaching—its goals, its authority, and its function within the small church. It is our contention that the members of the small church must claim the preaching office as a primary duty of their pastor and must claim the small church as an appropriate setting for truly great preaching.

What is *great* preaching? Who are the *great* preachers? John K. Bergland asked a number of small churches, and here is a summary of the responses he received.

1. Great preachers attract great crowds. Names like Roberts, Graham, Peale, Sheen, and Falwell come to mind. The television preachers have become the models for homiletical success. They preach to millions every week. Great preaching draws a great crowd; it is a box-office success.

2. Great preachers do great things to people. Great preaching elicits a distinct mood from a crowd. The preacher can be as witty and charming as a stand-up comedian or as dramatic and emotional as a Broadway actor. Great preaching affects people; it is an emotional success.

3. Great preachers impress us with their creativity. They combine original insights with literary excellence and rhetorical skill, to help us see old things in new ways. They give us important, imaginative, interesting things to think about. Great preaching is an artistic masterpiece.

Evidently, judging from these responses, the chief criterion for great preachers and great preaching is magnitude—great numbers of listeners, great feelings induced in the listeners, great thoughts imparted to the listeners. The test of this preaching is the listeners' test. The great preacher is the one who preaches to and for the great crowd.

103

When criteria like these are used to judge good preaching, it is easy to understand why the preacher in a small congregation, preaching to tens, rather than to thousands, feels defeated before the sermon begins. One need only "count the house" to see the obvious inadequacy of the preacher and the preaching.

One can also understand why such traditional homiletical standards as faithfulness to scripture, to the church's tradition, to orthodox theology, to prophetic social witness, and so forth, are jettisoned by many modern preachers. Apparently the sole proof of a good sermon is in the crowd—its size, its feelings, and its thoughts.

We would ask, Is it possible for preachers to serve the Word, to preach the gospel faithfully, to be responsible to their ordination, if the crowd is the main judge of preaching?

The only source of authority for the Christian preacher —the only authoritative basis for good *Christian* preaching—is theological. Service to the Word, not to the pleasure of the crowd, is the task to which the preacher is called. By envisioning preaching as standing before a crowd, rather than as standing under the Word, its authority has become domesticated, defused, and dissipated. No matter how "successful" the sermon may appear, if it offers anything other than the gospel, it has failed. And the preacher can never know, by asking the crowd, whether the proclamation presented was the gospel.

The two fundamental weaknesses of contemporary Protestant preaching—moralizing and psychologizing—are the results of misplaced homiletical authority.

Moralizing occurs when preachers pick through the biblical tradition in hope of finding texts from which to draw simple moral inferences, usually ideals that the listeners should do or be. The gospel is presented in the form of suggestions for better living, principles for correct opinion, or obligations to be met. In moralizing, the gospel is usually distorted by the pastor's earnest attempt to find something relevant to say—some easy, straightforward plan of action to urge upon the people. Moralizing perverts Christian proclamation, because the gospel usually has to do with *God's* actions and plans, rather than ours.

Psychologizing occurs when preachers impose our twentieth-century, psychologically oriented self-infatuation upon the gospel and come forth with a set of principles, programs, or general advice guaranteed to make the listener feel better. Popular preachers such as Oral Roberts, Robert Shuller, and Norman Vincent Peale have perfected this homiletical style. This preaching appeals to those of us who have been labeled the "me generation" and "psychological men"—those of us whose main project in life is the development, exploration, and care of our inner feelings, moods, and self-images. In such preaching, the gospel is distorted into an individualized, egocentric technique for self-fulfillment and self-gratification. The self-perceived needs of the listener are the preacher's primary concern.

We would argue that the supreme test for good preaching is faithfulness to the Word. Neither the size nor the attributes of the audience can measure a Christian sermon. Small-church preachers who are serious about their commission to preach the gospel are forced, by the small number of listeners, to look elsewhere than at the size of the crowd for authority in preaching. This is to their advantage. The hope we expressed earlier about worship

105

renewal, we now repeat concerning a renaissance in preaching: if there is to be a renewal, it may come first in the small church, simply because preachers in these churches are less likely to be diverted from the true purpose and authority of Christian preaching.

Service of the Word

The Christian preacher is, in H. H. Farmer's memorable phrase, a "Servant of the Word." Dynamic preaching occurs when the messenger has been grasped by the message. Whenever the preacher is not grasped by the message, he becomes what Paul once called a peddler—a huckster of a religious commodity to be marketed as glamorously as possible. The message (the gospel) creates the medium (the preacher); if it does not, the medium becomes the message, stands in the way of the gospel, and offers himself, rather than Christ. The evangelist is never as significant as the evangel. Preaching is powerful only when the preacher has something compelling to say. The problem in preaching is a theological/biblical problem, rather than one of communication. The need of the preacher is for theological clarity and consistency, and humble, skillful attentiveness to the testimony of the Bible. If the preacher steps into the pulpit looking for self-fulfillment, institutional affirmation, praise or blame from the system, or the adulation of the congregation, there is little likelihood that the Word will be faithfully served.

To advocate service to the Word as the primary function of Christian preaching is not to set theological concerns in opposition to pastoral concerns. It has been our observation that preachers who fulfill their task in the faithful, honest, humble, courageous serving of the Word, find that in so doing, they and their congregations are best

106

served. Preachers who play to the crowd or who work from a "star" image, are doomed to continuing frustration and failure, if they remain in the pulpits of small churches. The small congregation that continues to judge good preaching by the kind of showmanship and mass pep-rally approach it sees on television, in evangelistic crusades, or in the luminous pulpits of downtown cathedrals, is doomed to a continuing sense of inadequacy when it evaluates the preaching within its little parish. But the small-church pastor and congregation who develop a fascination for the Word, a genuine curiosity about the relation of treasured biblical tradition to contemporary questions, a joy in hearing the gospel story told so that it is recognizable as *the* story which is also *our* story—these preachers and congregations are well on their way to a significant rediscovery of preaching.

Contemporary preaching suffers because it has failed to steadily and earnestly engage the Bible. Preachers are misled into thinking that congregations want a personal testimony from them, rather than a witness to the testimony of the church, its scripture, and its tradition. As a result, the people flounder upon the preacher's own limited ideas, or efforts to win support for the denomination's latest social crusade, or rewording of the opinions put forth in current fads. The family suffers from amnesia; it forgets who it is and Whose it is; it loses its identity. The pastor loses the legitimate source of authority and anxiously searches for something new and clever to preach. The gospel becomes indistinguishable from the myriad of self-help techniques, "pop" psychologies, and programs for social betterment that the world sells at any given moment. The congregation is rarely judged, or corrected, or challenged. Both preacher and congregation

107

pathetically search for cheap self-affirmation and super-ficial mutual admiration, because they no longer hear the strong Word of God's grace. Little wonder that every renewal of Christianity has been accompanied by a rediscovery of biblical preaching.

Preachers on television and in immense city churches may be great rhetoricians; occasionally, they may be great expositors of the Word. But they will never be great servants of the Word, because they lack the pastoral, day-to-day encounters with the total life of God's people, which is a prerequisite for faithfulness to the Word. The Word is not some set of abstract principles addressed to humanity in general. The Word is not some self-contained, ancient object, once spoken and now lovingly protected and carefully reiterated. The Word arises out of the family's book (the Bible) and is enlivened and given concreteness in the context of the family's meetings (worship). Outside the gathered family, the Word doesn't make much sense. In the small church, where the preacher, known by the congregation, stands before a congregation known by the preacher, and where it is apparent that this is a family, gathering before the riches of their Book, and that the Word that is spoken is understood to be the contemporary family's Word, great preaching begins. The day-to-day struggles of the family can be claimed and set beside the Word with a solidarity, an intimacy, and a directness that is impossible in larger families. In such times, preaching becomes pastoral care—a continuing dialogue between a specific people with their God, who has called them forth. The preacher who has been at the bedside of the sick; who knows where the people work, where they hurt, where they spend their money, and make their lives; who feels charged by the community with the two-fold task of faithful listening to the people and to the Word—that preacher who has listened skillfully and conscientiously, Monday through Saturday, will have much worth saying when he or she preaches on Sunday. By serving the Word, the preacher will have dutifully served the family of God that stands under the Word, longing to hear that Word so that it may be obedient to it. The family patiently waits, and expectantly asks, as the preacher mounts the pulpit each Sunday, Is there any Word from the Lord?

The joy of faithfully receiving the Word of God, and of faithfully relating that Word to God's family, is the joy of preaching in the small-membership church.

Chapter Nine
Lay Reaction to Preaching: Receiving the Word

Preaching involves two participants: the preacher and the listener. While faithfulness to the Word is the first test of good preaching, it is also fair to ask how adequately the Word is being presented. Presumably the preacher knows what he or she is trying to communicate, but there may be some question as to whether the listener is receiving the message the minister is attempting to deliver. Every preacher from time to time is troubled by the thought, Are the people really listening?

This chapter is based in part on research in the area of lay reaction to preaching in small churches, conducted by Dr. John K. Bergland of Duke Divinity School. Included in that study was a questionnaire to be completed by lay persons at the conclusion of a service, giving their evaluation of the sermon. In one group of churches, the congregations were asked to evaluate the sermons on each of six consecutive Sundays. A number of judicatory lay officials also were enlisted to attend services in several small-membership churches, to assess the sermons. Pastors and lay persons were interviewed to secure their opinions about preaching. Congregations located in all parts of the country and affiliated with several Protestant denominations were included. While not a random sampling of small churches, those included are representative of such congregations. Some of the findings on the reactions of the people in the pews to the sermons they heard will be presented.

Is Anybody Listening?

The most important point the data confirm is that the people *are* listening to what the preachers say. Many ministers, however, are not convinced of this fact. In talking with pastors about their churches and about what they perceive to be the important and effective aspects of their ministry, preaching is rarely mentioned. The starting of new congregational programs, the remodeling or erection of buildings, and community service activities, all seem to be valued more highly than preaching.

The lay people tend not to let the preacher know how they feel about the sermon. The polite "I enjoyed your sermon, Reverend" that the pastor often receives at the end of the service is hardly conclusive evidence that the parishioners are really hearing what is said. Nevertheless, the people who gather faithfully in the pews Sunday after Sunday are in fact listening, hearing, and relating, to what the preacher says. For the people in the pews of Protestant churches, the sermon is still the most important event, and whether the clergy believe it or not, what they say has an impact on the lives of the listeners. It is almost impossible to find a group of lay people who, when asked to rate, in order of priority, all the tasks a minister is expected to perform, will not rate preaching somewhere near the top.

Recent understandings of the church have tended to downgrade preaching. The emphasis on the primary importance of community service and social action may lead some clergy to feel that virtually everything else is more important than leading worship and preaching. Pastors often tend to feel guilty when they are not engaged in some kind of church activity other than studying and preparing sermons. Very rarely is the parishioner who calls the church office or parsonage told that the minister is unavailable because he or she is preparing the sermon for next Sunday. It is, of course, perfectly legitimate for a caller to be told that the minister is making a pastoral call, participating in some community activity, or attending a meeting at the denominational headquarters. In fact, we noted time and again that some pastors allow almost anything to interrupt their study and sermon preparation. The congregation perceives that when the pastor is busy doing the work of the church (and presumably the work of the Lord), he or she is engaged in some type of organizational or community activity—certainly not spending time in prayer, meditation, and study, in preparation for next Sunday's sermon. One is surprised that lay persons take the sermon as seriously as they do, when many clergy seem to give it less than top priority.

Several reasons can be suggested for ministers' underinvestment in preaching. One cause may be the expectation of the denominations that the pastor should give priority to participation in service-type activities outside the congregation. Another is the mandated organizational machinery that requires the time and attention of pastors.

Preaching is difficult, requiring time and self-discipline. It is easier to busy oneself with routine, time-consuming, but less demanding, administrative tasks. Preaching requires ministers to expose their faith—and doubts—to the congregations. It is impossible for them to preach week after week to small congregations of people whom they know and who know them, without the risk of laying their personal faith on the line. This is perhaps the most difficult aspect of preaching.

The studies of reactions to sermons in small churches also revealed that lay people are extremely reluctant to be

112

critical of preaching. They are not only hesitant to criticize their own pastor's sermons, but they tend not to want to be critical of sermons of other pastors in the same, or even in different, denominations. There is a kind of halo effect around the ordained minister; he or she is someone who is presumed to have been called by God. While the minister is not perceived as someone who can do no wrong (people are always willing to gossip about the shortcomings of community leaders, including pastors), the members of the congregation do not want to make their negative feelings known to their minister. If the sermon is particularly vague on a certain Sunday morning, they may excuse it by saying that they simply did not understand the finer points of theology the minister must have been attempting to make. "He may not be the greatest preacher in the world, but he is a wonderful pastor," they may say as they rationalize homiletical incompetence. There seems to be a feeling that to criticize the minister is a little bit like criticizing God; it simply isn't done.

Another reason lay people are reluctant to be critical of sermons is that to do so would reflect negatively on their church. Members tend to have an intense loyalty to their local congregation, and they want to be proud of it. To draw attention to its shortcomings or any weakness of the pastor is a reflection on themselves. They employ the pastor and pay his or her salary. If their minister is not performing adequately, a major share of the responsibility to remedy the situation is theirs. It is less threatening to avoid these issues by simply accepting uncritically what the pastor says.

Despite the refusal of many lay people to be critical of their clergy, there is evidence that the hearers are evaluating and reacting to the preaching. In an interview, when they are pushed, they finally admit that the point of the sermon was in fact vague, and maybe—just maybe—it wasn't their lack of theological sophistication that made understanding it impossible. They may also express bafflement that their preacher seems to find so little time to be adequately prepared in the pulpit.

When a pastor himself asks for criticism of the sermons, the people are at first reluctant to give it. They aren't sure the minister really wants their reactions. Therefore, the initial verbalized response will tend to be positive. However, as time passes, and the people understand that the pastor really wants a critical response, they will become more negative. They will get up enough nerve to say what they actually mean. Thus the pastor who manages to persuade the people to criticize the sermons over a period of a month or two should be prepared for increasingly truthful, and possibly negative, responses.

The minister who really wants a critique of the sermon can get it. A short, simple questionnaire for laity can be devised. If this is used over a period of time, the people will give honest reactions. Some pastors have had informal sessions with their members to talk about the sermon. It takes some time for the people to learn that the minister wants honest criticism. However, when they decide the minister genuinely values their reactions, church members will oblige.

Lay people know a bad sermon when they hear one. A part of the mentioned research involved having all persons present in a group of churches fill out an evaluation form at the conclusion of each service, over a six-week period. There tended to be a high degree of agreement. When the sermon on a particular Sunday left something to be desired, most hearers agreed and rated it lower. While the people were reluctant to call a sermon poor, there tended to be a consensus on certain Sundays that the quality had dropped; the ratings on such days would decline from excellent to good, or fair. While the church members didn't want to sound too negative, they seemed to be discerning about the sermons they were hearing.

Lay Persons' Expectations

Even if lay persons in local churches tend to be reluctant to be openly critical of the sermon, they seem to have some fairly clear ideas of what constitutes a good sermon. As part of the research on reactions to sermons, lay people were given a list of twenty-two items which described a sermon and were asked to check the five they felt were most important. They were not asked to list these in order of priority, but simply to select those five they felt were most desirable. There was general unanimity on three characteristics, among those who listen to preaching in small congregations, week after week.

Most people indicated that an important characteristic of a sermon is that it be "faithful to scripture." Almost as frequently designated by large numbers of church people were two other qualities: "preached with authority" and "sincerely believed by the preacher."

There is in Protestantism a tradition, and apparently a continuing expectation, that sermons should be biblically based—that they should be faithful to scripture. This does not mean that church members accept the Bible as a literal guide for their behavior. The pastor who stands in the pulpit on Sunday morning and tells the congregation that because the Bible says something it is true and that they should act accordingly, knows that these words will not necessarily be believed or heeded. Many pastors have had

115

the experience of preaching a biblically sound sermon, the product of careful exegesis, only to have the people's response indicate that this sermon was the most boring one they ever heard. The Bible says many things that contemporary church members dismiss as being irrelevant, a product of the culture of the times in which the scripture was written, a word which may have applied to someone at some time, but which no longer applies to us. One only need consider the biblical injunction against divorce, to have an example of this phenomenon. The women's movement is reinterpreting parts of scripture relative to the role of women in the church. Therefore, lay people, while almost unanimously indicating that their preachers should be "faithful to scripture," quite obviously do not accept the Bible alone as the ultimate authority.

The next two most desired characteristics of a sermon shed light on this apparent contradiction—desiring a sermon to be faithful to the scriptures, while ignoring certain biblical teachings. Lay people want their sermons to be "preached with authority" and they want them to be "sincerely believed by the preacher." What we seem to have is the expectation that the Christian tradition, as set forth in scripture, will be filtered through the interpretation of a pastor who has a deep and sincere faith—who really believes what he or she is saying. Preaching is given a sense of authority when the scripture is interpreted by a minister who has wrestled with the fundamental religious issues and the basic tradition, and who has had personal experience with the difficulty of living in contemporary society. Out of such experience, a preacher is able to express the relevance of the scripture for the everyday lives of the listeners. The people are saying that they want preaching based on the authority of the scripture, reinforced by the authority of the personal experience of a pastor who has a sincere and deep faith. The authority of preaching is biblical, but only insofar as preaching represents the pastor's personal, experiential, confrontation with the Bible.

This is no easy task. It places an awesome responsibility upon the minister. It also indicates that the lay people do in fact have some understanding of what preaching is all about—that they see good preaching occurring when a person of faith interprets the Word with authority, in a manner applicable to life.

Reaction to the Total Person

It is axiomatic that the reaction to a sermon is a reaction to the total person. If church members do not have confidence in the pastor, it is unlikely that they will have confidence in his or her sermons. Conversely, the congregation that trusts its minister may follow that leadership, even when they are not quite sure they want to be going in that particular direction.

The preacher in the small church can claim and develop this personal base for homiletical authority. In the small church, the people come to know their minister well, often much more so than in a large congregation. Consequently, the reaction to the preaching in the small church will be largely a reaction to the pastor as a total person. In the large congregation, it is possible that many of the people in the Sunday morning service do not know the pastor intimately. Their contact may be limited to the more formal relationship that exists in a large social group. This would suggest to us that the preacher who desires to communicate the biblical Word with personal authority, and with

117

his or her total personality, is under a great disadvantage in a large, detached congregation.

It is easier to ignore prophetic preaching in a large church. When the pastor of a small congregation takes a stand or preaches a sermon on a controversial or prophetic theme, the listeners must react to an individual whom they know well. More than likely, they know that the one who makes these pronouncements is one who shares some of their own strengths and weaknesses. It is much harder to reject the arguments of someone who is perceived as a close friend, or even as a member of the family, than those of an individual who is an outsider. There are few hiding places in the small church. The Word comes with a directness, intimacy, and personality that makes hiding difficult.

This task places a heavy responsibility on the preacher in the church of small membership. Not only does he or she have the duty to proclaim the Word, but of doing so within an intimate family-like group, to people who know, and are well known by, the minister. In no other setting does preaching have the potential of exerting greater influence on the lives of the listeners.

Chapter Ten
Servants of the Word

To be a Christian is not easy. Those who elect to follow the Christ have demands placed on them that require dedication, discipline, and sacrifice. Those who accept an office in the congregation assume greater responsibility for the ministry of the church than does the average member. Those who become ordained ministers enter a demanding profession; to proclaim the Word of God is an awesome task.

The ministry of the church is the responsibility of both the laity and the clergy. Nowhere is this more evident than in the small congregation, where a large portion of the people participate in the management and ministry of the church. In this concluding chapter we shall focus on the role of the leaders, both lay and clergy, of preaching and worship in the small church.

Be What You Are

Throughout this book we have argued that the church of small membership can be an effective instrument for ministry, particularly for preaching and worship. Whatever else a congregation may or may not do, preaching the Word and participating in worship are essential, if the group is to be a Christian church. In emphasizing what small churches cannot do, what such churches *can* do well (i.e., preaching and worship) is too frequently neglected.

The small size of a congregation, of course, does not

guarantee that it will provide effective preaching and worship, or that it will be supportive, understanding, and open. These characteristics are the result of the members' personal values and their understanding of themselves as a Christian congregation. The fact that there are fewer members simply provides certain opportunities and limitations, different from those of a larger church, for carrying out the congregation's ministry.

The opportunities within the small church do not exempt it from certain institutional limitations imposed by its size. And it is at this point that ministers may experience their greatest frustrations. The clergy has a major responsibility for the efficient operation of the local church, including securing adequate funds for necessary expenses and for the congregation's share of the denominational overhead and benevolence programs. Because the number of contributors is limited, lack of funds is a perennial problem.

Many small churches, because of such factors as the modest salaries they can provide and the low prestige associated with serving such congregations, may not be blessed with the most experienced or best pastors and worship leaders. Many tend to be fairly young or fairly old, with whatever strengths or weaknesses that entails. Also, the small church will generally have to share its minister with one or more other congregations, thus having to make do with a part-time pastor.

These and other perplexing problems caused by smallness will persist. The small church can never carry out the full program designed by the denominational bureaucrats. But the primary task of a congregation is not to fit into some predetermined institutional pattern or

120

even to provide for the clergy, but to worship and to hear the Word. This the small church can do, and do well, provided it is willing to be what it is and does not expend its energy trying unsuccessfully to be what it cannot become.

"But," someone is certain to say, "we can't have a church unless we have enough people to employ a pastor, raise a budget, maintain a building, and have a full church program." To this, the reply is that the function of the church is to proclaim the Word, administer the sacraments, and worship. All else, however useful and desirable, is secondary.

Expect, and You May Receive

Preaching and worship are responsibilities usually left to the clergy. It is assumed that pastors have received training in these areas while they were in theological seminary and that they are competent in both fields. As has been pointed out, lay persons are reluctant to be critical of sermons. They simply do not let their ministers know what they really think of the preaching they hear and the worship they experience week after week.

The clergy will take preaching and worship more seriously when the laity make it clear that they expect their pastors to do so. Here again, the churches of small membership provide an excellent setting for this to occur. The informal setting of the small church provides opportunities for many of the members to discuss the worship services and the sermons with the pastor, at times and in approaches that are not possible in large congregations.

The critical factor is the people's willingness to let their ministers know what they really think about what is taking

121

place on Sunday morning, even at the risk of hurting the pastor's feelings. The members, particularly the leaders of the congregations, owe it to themselves and to their pastors to make their true opinions known.

For the laity to share their feelings about preaching and worship is their first step in the development of a sense of responsibility for these aspects of the church's ministry. It can lead them to a better understanding of these functions. It can raise the congregations' expectations and cause many pastors to give preaching and worship the priority they merit. And it can lead to a larger role for lay people in the planning and leading of worship.

Better communication between laity and clergy can help the church members more readily grasp the difficulties and very real frustrations of the ministry, and the external pressures under which pastors work. If the lay people shared their feelings, the ministers probably would, also. Lay people would then be more understanding and supportive of their pastors and their families. They would affirm the very many things the church of small membership *can* do, rather than lament what it cannot do.

The Measure of Success

Preaching and worship have been and continue to be the particular tasks of the pastor. Despite the desirability of lay participation in the planning and leading of worship, the pastor must continue to carry the major responsibility for what happens on Sunday morning.

The central tasks of the minister are to proclaim the Word and to lead worship. The preacher therefore occupies a unique role as a servant of the Word—the one who stands before the congregation each week to proclaim the message from the Lord. The joy of preaching comes from the preacher's realization that he or she is in fact the servant of the Word. The knowledge that the Word was faithfully proclaimed and that the congregation worshiped God must be justification enough for the minister's efforts.

The pastor who accepts the prevailing cultural standards of size and growth as the criteria of success will have difficulty in the small church. There will not be large crowds to participate in worship and hear the sermon. There will not be the full church program or the local church organization the denominational bureaucracy sees as essential. There will not be funds to make the requested contributions to the denomination's benevolent projects. If these are the standards of accomplishment, we can predict little more than continuing frustration and a sense of inadequacy for the pastor.

To the pastor who is serving or who may serve a church of small membership, we have a final word. If you measure the success of your ministry by the size of the crowd, the prestige of the church you serve, or the praise of the denominational authorities, you are in deep trouble in the small church.

But if you sense that you are called of God—if you know that your ultimate authority and the final validation of your ministry come from the faithful service and celebration of the Word and its confrontation by God's people, your servanthood will continue to be blessed. You will have the joy of knowing that you are faithfully proclaiming the Word, and that you are an instrument of God's grace for the people who worship in a church of small membership.

Almighty God,

Who asks nothing more nor less from us than ceaseless praise and enjoyment of your presence in our world

Who sets in our hearts the love of your kingdom and the hope of its fulfillment

Who gives us the Christ, one like us, come into our midst to reveal your love and your way for us—

Christ,

Who promised us that where only two or three gather in his name, there he will be also

Who brought us into your family by water and Spirit

Who was made known to us in the breaking of bread

Who showed us a God who cares deeply for the one lost sheep, the one lost coin, and the one lost boy, the lilies of the field, the things the world judges to be small and insignificant

Who called each of us by name, who gave us your family in which to belong and a task to do in your Kingdom—

Bless, we pray, all those who labor for the gospel, all those whose lives and deeds faithfully witness to your love among us, that they may not weary in their efforts to serve you and your Word; so that, by their ministry and mission, your family might be perfected and your kingdom advanced.

Through Jesus Christ our Lord,

Amen

Suggestions for Further Reading

Bailey, Wilfred M. *Awakened Worship.* Nashville: Abingdon, 1972.

Carroll, Jackson W., ed. *Small Churches Are Beautiful.* New York: Harper & Row, 1977.

Dudley, Carl S. *Making the Small Church Effective.* Nashville: Abingdon, 1978.

Hovda, Robert W. *Strong, Loving, and Wise; Presiding in Liturgy.* The Liturgical Conference, 1976.

Johnson, Merle A. *How to Be Happy in the Non-Electric Church:* Nashville: Abingdon, 1979.

Kay, Melissa, ed. *It is Your Own Mystery: A Guide to the Communion Rite.* The Liturgical Conference, 1977.

Keck, Leander E. *The Bible in the Pulpit.* Nashville: Abingdon, 1978.

Madsen, Paul O. *The Small Church; Valid, Vital, Victorious.* Valley Forge, Pa.: Judson Press, 1975.

Mitchell, Leonel L. *The Meaning of Ritual.* Paramus, N.J.: Paulist Press, 1977.

Seasons of the Gospel. Nashville: Abingdon, 1979. Contains lectionary.

Senn, Frank C. *The Pastor as Worship Leader.* Minneapolis: Augsburg, 1977.

A Service of Christian Marriage. Nashville: Abingdon, 1979.

A Service of Death and Resurrection. Nashville: Abingdon, 1979.

White, James F. *Introduction: to Christian Worship.* Nashville: Abingdon, 1980.

Willimon, William H. *Word, Water, Wine, and Bread.* Valley Forge, Pa.: Judson Press, 1980.

Willimon, William H. *Worship as Pastoral Care.* Nashville: Abingdon, 1979.

Word and Table: A Basic Pattern of Sunday Worship. Nashville: Abingdon, 1976. Contains lectionary.

CREATIVE LEADERSHIP SERIES
Edited by Lyle E. Schaller

Books to provide practical help in developing and administering a more effective church program, for both lay and clergy leaders

Please send me the following books:

—*Assimilating New Members* by Lyle E. Schaller
  01938-9
—*Beginning a New Pastorate* by Robert G. Kemper
  02750-0
—*Building an Effective Youth Ministry* by Glenn E. Ludwig
  03992-4
—*The Care and Feeding of Volunteers* by Douglas W. Johnson
  04669-6
—*Church Growth* by Donald McGavran and George Hunter
  08160-2
—*Creative Stewardship* by Richard B. Cunningham
  09844-0
—*Leading Churches Through Change* by Douglas Alan Walrath
  21270-7
—*Preaching and Worship in the Small Church* by William H. Willimon and Robert L. Wilson
  33820-4
—*Time Management* by Speed B. Leas
  42120-9
—*Your Church Can Be Healthy* by C. Peter Wagner
  46870-1

$4.95, paper/each book

MAIL ENTIRE PAGE TO:

Customer Service Manager * Abingdon * 201 Eighth Avenue, South * Nashville, TN 37202
Send books checked to

Name_____
            (Please print or type)

Address_____

City_____State_____Zip_____

I am enclosing $_____(plus 65¢ to cover postage and handling).
*Please send check or money order—no cash or C.O.D. accepted.
*Please allow three weeks for delivery.